Come Back Home

Finding The Love We Lost

Jeannie Remy

The following translations of the Bible were used for scriptures quoted in this book:

Amplified Bible, Classic Edition (AMPC)
New Living Translation (NLT)
New International Version (NIV)
English Standard Version (ESV)

Dedication

<u>To My Husband Mike,</u>

I don't even know where to begin to thank you for believing in me during every step of my journey and allowing God's plan to flourish. Your patience, love, and support played a vital role in the outcome of this book and my mission to share our story. I couldn't have done it without your complete understanding, knowing this is what I've been called to do. I love you more than words can ever express; you are my greatest gift from God, and I am so blessed to have you as my husband.

<u>To My Son Connor,</u>

Thank you for your time and patience in helping me with the technical aspects needed to write this book. I know this was a great challenge to repeatedly show me things you had already taught me. You witnessed my mistakes, especially the one where I erased my work, and watched me cry at the thought of having to do it all over again. These trying moments were not fun for any of us, but God knew that technology was certainly not my strong point, and I needed your knowledge to see me through it all. I love you and am so blessed to have you as my son.

To My Daughter Shannon,

Thank you from the bottom of my heart for believing in me and giving me another chance to be the kind of mother that I have always wanted to be. Our relationship has become the kind of story that most mothers and daughters only dream of having. I am so grateful for your love and am looking forward to God's next great plan for our future. I love you and am so blessed to have you as my daughter. You are a light in so many people's lives, and I know your time to shine to the rest of the world is coming.

To Sammy Maloof,

I am profoundly grateful for your mentorship, and the incredible blessing that you've been in my life. I have been forever changed by the wave of events that occurred along the course of this journey. You have played a crucially important role in the changes that have taken place in my family's lives. Your great wisdom shed light on the truth to conquer my life's trials. You saw me through the eyes of God and believed in me when I had no hope. You have been a major inspiration that led me to share my success with others. I love you and thank God for the privilege of having you as my mentor to help me see the light at the end of the tunnel.

<u>A Special Thanks to John Heart and Janeen Ferdinand,</u>

John, I know that you are a humble man of God, but I hope you understand the important role you played in my life. Your genuine pursuit to extend your kindness and love to me, when I was completely lost, was the impetuous for the necessary changes in all our lives. You were an essential key that brought this story to light. I love you and will never forget how important you are to me.

Janeen, I need to thank you especially for being such a strong influence in my daughter's life and giving her hope. You are so beautifully talented and gifted as a singer. The song you sang, "Mary Did You Know" touched her so deeply. It literally helped to save her when she was lost and at the end of her rope. You played an essential part in mentoring her in music and helping her to discover her true talents. From one mother to another, I love you and thank you for caring for her when I could not. I thank God for you and will never forget how special you are to me.

<u>To All My Fellow Christian Brothers and Sisters, Writers and Teachers,</u>

I am so grateful to all of you who played a significant role in the shaping of my life by helping me to know God's truth.

<u>And Most Importantly to My Lord and Savior Jesus,</u>

Thank you for your unfathomable love and bringing me back to you. Thank you for sending all these amazing people into my life, who have taken part to help our family when we needed it most and thank you for helping me to persevere under the many pressures it took to complete my mission to write our story. We have been blessed beyond measure to have chosen our faith in You for our family's complete restoration. Even when I wanted to give up, God gave me the strength to hold on.

Introduction

The devastation of my daughter's disappearance, along with the realization of my own deep-rooted lack of fulfillment, caused my life to feel as if it had suddenly fallen apart. She and I were both misguided and were looking for direction in our lives. Along the way, we found the missing pieces through our faith and fellowship with God.

Although we appeared to be the perfect family on the outside, we were breaking apart on the inside. I believed that I could hold it all together on my own, falsely believing I could cover up all the lies, deceits, and torture of feeling unfulfilled by not speaking about it. Looking back, I realized the misery that was seeping out of me was destroying my life and family.

I will take you through my walk of faith as it unfolded and how it became the most eye-opening experience of my life. As God revealed each personal change that I so desperately needed to make, my elusive true desires were finally uncovered. Consequently, I began experiencing unimaginable new paths in my life which filled the empty places of my heart.

The lessons learned through my hardships showed me how to have a joyful and fulfilled life, even during the most challenging circumstances. I learned to live in constant hope, knowing anything is possible with God. During this process, He has inspired me to share my personal life's struggles and victories. Throughout my story, you will witness the power of faith, and how it can transform anyone's life, including their family's future for generations to come.

Along this journey, I discovered many challenges amongst all my hidden realities that I was not sure I could face. I was given the choice to either continue to live with the pain of feeling unfulfilled, or to work through the pain of change to get to the other side.

I learned to rise above these challenges by having the right attitude and proper thoughts, combined with the will to never give up. Meditating on the Word of God and applying it to each obstacle which blocked my healing process was ultimately what brought me victory. Throughout this journey, my life evolved with love, joy, peace, and personal fulfillment.

With one step at a time, God released me from the heavy chains which held me back from living my life to the fullest. I was given new hope and the belief that it is never too late for change. Through my walk of faith, the lives of both my family and I were restored. We experienced God's grace and mercy, and accepted the opportunities for spiritual growth, which cultivated a new foundation of inner strength that was lacking in each of our lives before.

I share this journey with the explicit details of my own personal failures. Through my own experience of success, I hope to be able to help others who are suffering in their own lives. God has placed this desire in my heart, and without any formal experience in writing has given me the ability to express all that has unfolded in my life within this book.

Prior to this journey, I was lost without any direction or knowing what reason I had for waking up in the morning. God has changed me into a woman with a renewed passion for living and has given me an immeasurable amount of belief in myself to do what I never would have done without Him. This story will take you through the depths of my life changing relationship with Him, from my most intimate experiences of worship to the transformations of perspective I needed to finally find out who I truly was. From being lost from myself, my family and God, I have finally come back home to find the blessing of a fulfilled life greater than I ever imagined.

Chapter 1

The Wakeup Call

Over a period of eighteen years, I lived the so-called perfect life as a wife and a stay-at-home mother. This was all I ever dreamed of being since I was a little girl. To the best of my abilities, I spent every day making sure that my family's basic needs were met. However, over the years, I noticed a constant state of restlessness, somewhere deep inside my heart. As the years went on, the stirring inside of me only seemed to escalate and created a troubled sense of unhappiness. Without addressing this issue properly, it began spiraling out of control, and landed me straight into a pit of bitterness and resentment. Without knowing what to do, I began shutting down emotionally. This pain caused me to build walls, which isolated me away from most everyone in my life. Consequently, I closed myself off from any possibility of having open and honest communication. My unhappiness became the center of all the problems that would then arise, not only for me, but for my family as well.

On August 20th, 2013, I was struck with the sudden reality of my teenage daughter's disappearance. Later that night, I found only a letter informing us that she had run away from home in search of her dream life. She vanished from our lives and left us all behind, not only to pick up her broken pieces, but the broken pieces of our own hearts as well. She spent years planning her trip, never telling us anything about it until the day she left. I had nothing more than a letter with so little words, explaining her reasons for leaving. Only a vague description of her departure was explained in her letter. She was leaving for a journey that was calling her heart for quite some time. In this letter, she informed us there would be no way of contacting her, since she discarded her cellphone. She briefly explained all her reasons for being so selfish. Yet, having this inner voice telling her to go anyway, she explained it was just something she had to do. The letter stated that she was chasing a dream, and it was the reason she woke up every morning. She felt it was a great adventure that we never would have allowed her to go on. She claimed this was her main reason for not telling us anything about it.

As I read her letter in disbelief, I was overcome with a paralyzing sense of grief. I wondered how it was ever possible that I was unaware of her secret life of schemes. How could my child have made such a heartless decision without realizing it would have left me feeling torn apart inside? I was not only left with her drastic absence, but I had no idea where she was going, or what reasons she had for leaving in such a cold-hearted way. My imagination ran wild and tormented me every second since I realized she was gone. I didn't have any idea about the dreams she held onto, and I felt completely cut off from her life. I couldn't seem to wrap my mind around what had suddenly happened. Knowing her warm and loving heart, none of this made any sense to me. She never gave me a day of trouble in her entire life, and this was completely out of character for her. I felt this secret, pre-meditated way of leaving was the ultimate form of betrayal. Knowing my child, I just couldn't fathom that she would make such a heartless choice, unless it was under the dark influence of others.

I was the only one at the time, who wasn't willing to pull the wool over my eyes about the way she left. I needed to find the root of the problems which caused her to make such a decision without us. I felt extreme guilt knowing she grew up and witnessed my unhappiness and knew that it somehow played a part in this overall mess. I was overcome with my emotions as the reality of her letter began sinking in. I felt at a complete loss not only for my daughter, but also for my own worth and reason for existence. My life's accumulation of failures had added up over the years, and her sudden disappearance from my life felt like the worst of them all.

As I reflected upon my role as her mother, I felt greatly responsible, knowing I wasn't there for her the way I should have been. I felt washed up, worn out, and my life felt completely out of control with the years of my unhappiness that stood between us. This moment was the absolute lowest point of my life, leaving me face to face with the circumstances. So many facets of my life were in a complete state of ruin. I felt there was no way out. I had about five minutes of feeling sunk under this crashing tide of emotions when suddenly, before my eyes, I saw a flash vision from God. In this vision, there were many changes that needed to be made in my life. I had to finally fix all my problems that were in desperate need of healing for so long. All the issues which had accumulated over the course of my life were being played out in my mind. I realized the way I was living my life was not nearly all God had planned for me. Nevertheless, God gave me a sense of assurance that He was going to show me how to fix it all. I felt that He was waiting for me all along, and in this moment of sorrow, my life would finally begin to change.

As I reflected upon my life, I was overwhelmed that I had allowed my unhappiness to spiral out of control. For years, I lived without ever addressing the issues that were causing my behaviors. I realized this had a very negative effect on my daughter's life and all my relationships. I spent years living with emptiness inside my heart, and in the moment of her runaway, it hit me harder than ever. As I thought back over the years, I realized my misery was the major contributor to the downfall in our lives. Because of this, I was left wondering if she was running from me, or for me. I questioned if her running away was an attempt to get away from my sadness, or was she trying to live out the dreams she knew I had failed to do in my own life?

Chapter 2

Taking a Stand

I woke up every day and lived my life as most people do, in the so-called normal scheme of things. I spent my days trying to convince myself I was happy and had it all. Somehow, I knew deep down inside something was missing along the way. As far back as I can recall, I had this feeling that no matter where I was, it wasn't where I really belonged. I felt I was acting out the wrong role in the scene of my own movie. As the years passed by, I settled into the thought that I needed to accept life just as it was. I believed I didn't deserve anything more than what I already had. This thought always left me with a yearning for more; I just didn't know exactly what it was.

Comparing myself to all the women I knew over the years, I realized most of them were just as unhappy as I was, if not more so. I told myself not to be ungrateful, and yet I was always coming up with a feeling of emptiness inside. I wondered if dropping my expectations of everyone would be a better resolution, only to find out I was left without any hope. It seemed nothing was even coming close to meeting any of my needs. Without any answers, I went on living my life just as everyone else does, by settling for less than what my heart truly desired.

Over the years, I tried desperately to help other women with their problems. I was always unsuccessful in my attempts. I didn't have the answers for them, nor myself, to resolve our unhappiness. We were all missing pieces in our lives. Although we could mutually identify them on the surface, we lacked the wisdom to get to the core of our problems. The answers for our never-ending problems, and the lack of our own fulfillment, eluded us. Nothing ever changed. Day in and day out we were only talking in circles, living a life of riddles.

Over the years, we were left with many failed attempts to fix our own lives. We were continually left within our own world of frustrations, not knowing what to do next. We were lost and hopeless and realized our marriages were failing. The children were in complete rebellion, the bills were adding up, and we were constantly feeling sick and tired of it all. The lives we led pulled us apart at the seams. Most of us were lost without any direction. This was the defining moment in which we all began to wonder why our anti-aging creams just weren't working anymore.

The years of life's stresses finally began catching up with us. Not only by the outward expression of our worn faces, but also by the inward torment of our own bitterness. Eventually, we were unable to hide what was living on the inside of us; and all the pieces of our lives were falling apart. We went on in our daily lives in constant struggle for the quest of how to find true and complete happiness. We searched for material possessions to fulfill our unmet needs. They were never enough. Always believing that our problems were in everyone and everything else, we never realized that the problems were within our own hearts.

There came a point at which I realized I could no longer hope for the answers by talking amongst fellow women, as I knew we did not have the solutions for our problems. Giving each other hope by finding the true answer to our problems became my vision and mission. I was willing to stand up and make changes in myself first; knowing one day it would also provide answers for many other women. I also wanted to use my life as an example for all parents. Even if a child doesn't necessarily pack a bag and runaway, they may be lost and looking for life's answers without having a reliable source. I witnessed many children being brought up with parents who settled for less in their own lives, just as I did. Our example fell short, denying our children the hope and faith to go beyond the barriers of our own limitations.

My daughter took a very dangerous path by running away in the hopes of finding herself. Her decision could have been avoided with the proper wisdom to make a better choice. I refused to chalk her behavior up to a normal course of rebellion. Without finding the root cause of her rebellion, I also would not have the answers for other parents. I could no longer accept living according to the world's standards. I promised God I would once and for all step up and be accountable for my own mess. It was from this point forward that healing my emotional and spiritual wounds became my first mission. I took it one step at a time, beginning with addressing the wounds in my heart. I meditated on Psalm 147:3, "He heals the brokenhearted and binds up their wounds {curing their pains and sorrows}." I began to allow God to heal the pains and sorrows I carried from my childhood. The chaotic state of own family led me to believe that my only choice was to allow God to make a message out of it. I didn't know where to begin, other than to seek God and change me, so I could become a better person for my family. I knew I had to be accountable for all the things I didn't do right. It was my responsibility to pursue God so that He could mend what was broken inside of me. Wasting no time, I took it step by step as I journeyed with God. It was through faith in Him that I believed my family could be restored, but I had to begin by allowing God to deal with my heart first.

The following months were spent humbling myself before the Lord as He revealed all that was lying underneath the years of my pain. The pain of change was not easy, but the pain of staying where I was had become unbearable. I was finished with making excuses for my unhappiness. I knew if not for myself, I had to at least find the strength to change for my daughter's sake. I knew my unhappiness played a part in her disappearance, and it affected her life, as negatively as my own.

The changes I needed to make were a fight that I had to press through. This was not only for myself and my family, but for the other families I wanted to help as well. The examples I set as a wife and mother needed to be renewed. I knew my daughter left because she sensed hopelessness inside of me. Once and for all, I was determined to change. Fulfilling my own life would set a new example not only for her, but for many others. I wanted my renewed life to set the way for many women by letting them know their lives can be fulfilled through the will of God. More than anything, I wanted my daughter back in my life, but unlike before. I wanted a new chance to become the mother and role model she could admire. My desire was to show her the changes I could make in myself. I needed this opportunity to make up for all that I previously neglected to do, and the Holy Spirit took me through the Word of God one step at a time to renew the state of my soul.

Chapter 3

Leaving Without a Trace

It seemed like the usual kind of day, as I went about my daily activities at home. Shannon was going off to work that day, or so I thought. She was wearing her work clothes with a knapsack on her back. I noticed it was packed to the brim; practically overflowing with what I thought was a change of clothes, and a mighty big towel.

Even though the over packed knapsack seemed strange to me, I didn't question what was in it. Previously, she never gave me any reason to question her whereabouts. Therefore, I trusted she wasn't doing anything out of the ordinary. Without any doubt in my mind, I said to her, "I guess you're going out with your friends after work tonight?" She looked me in the eyes and replied, "Maybe mom." As she proceeded to embrace me for an unusually long hug; it seemed out of the ordinary compared to our typically short and sweet kind of hug. It felt more like it was a goodbye, as if to say, "I'm not going to be seeing you for quite a while." By eleven thirty she hadn't come home that night, as was usually expected. I called her cell phone continuously without any answers. For some unexplainable reason, I was suddenly overcome with a strange feeling that she had run away. I tried to call her cell phone over the next few hours. With each passing hour, I realized her unusually long goodbye hug was about to become a dark reality, which would forever change our lives.

That evening, when she didn't return home from work, my fear escalated to heights that were unbearable to manage. I knew she was gone, I tried to open the door to her room, only to find she had locked it. I managed to unlock the door and rushed over to open her drawers to find out if her clothes were still in them. I looked through every draw only to find most of her clothes were missing. I knew in my heart wherever she went; she must have been long gone by this time.

At four in the morning, I woke up my husband Mike and told him I had been awake all night and she hadn't come home yet. I expressed my concern about having a strange feeling that she had run away. He kept trying to give me some reassurance by saying, "Jeannie, teenage kids want to stay all night, and you're just letting your imagination run wild. Try to be calm, we will find her. She probably fell asleep at a friend's house."

With the curfew I set for her, she never stayed out much past midnight unless she had an especially planned event. At six o'clock that morning Mike decided to drive around town to see if he could find her. During this time, I went back into her room to look around more thoroughly. I had no idea what I was looking for until I found a letter tucked deep in the corner of her desk. It was hidden behind her TV so that it was out of my immediate sight, until this time. I can remember my entire body felt numb as I slowly walked towards the letter.

Everything seemed to move in slow motion, as my mind thought of the worst-case scenarios, wondering what she wrote in her letter. I remember thinking for a second, "Oh God, I hope this is not a suicide letter!" My hands shook as I read the final words written in her letter, "I'm going away for a while. I love you and I will miss you." Her letter was so vague that it only left me thinking of the worst-case scenarios as to the reason she ran away!

My body froze in the chair and my heart was filled with utter sadness. Suddenly, I envisioned myself on a Dateline missing person interview, which I really didn't want to be in. The letter only briefly explained her departure and left me with the terror of so many unanswered questions. I felt my body's immediate reaction going into a shear panic. I had no idea how to control my level of anxiety, and my emotions went into a feeling of complete desperation to find out where she was headed.

Not long after reading her letter, the cold harsh reality began setting in. Everything I was living for as her mother completely vanished in that moment. I felt worthless and immediately began falling apart, as I questioned my ability as her mother. I thought I gave her everything I had from my heart and soul in loving her everyday up until this point. The moment I read her letter became the shocking finality that our lives were no longer together. It seemed unimaginable to me that my daughter's sudden departure became a heart-breaking reality for us as a family.

Suddenly remembering the moment, I hugged her goodbye, I knew deep down inside, that she was going somewhere far away. At the time, I had no idea about her runaway plan. I only remember a strange feeling that went through me so quickly but was incomprehensible at the time.

I knew something was out of the ordinary, and yet, I brushed it off as if it was just a crazy thought of my imagination. Later that night when she disappeared, I remembered this intuitive feeling during our unusually extended hug. I wished in that moment that I would have questioned all the belongings in her knapsack to avoid her from running away. For some unknown reason, I didn't say anything except "goodbye."

This was truly the moment that would become the wakeup call of my life. I only wished I would have hugged her longer that day, not having any idea it would be so long before I would see her again.

With the reality of her being gone, I was overcome with fear and not knowing what to do next. Mike checked our personal family files to discover that she took all her personal identification with her. I was immediately struck with the thought that she could have left the country! I quickly called the police department and filed a missing person's report. They placed her name on high alert for all buses, airports, trains, and port authorities. In the days that followed, I was

16

only left with the agony of waiting for a phone call from the police department.

Two sleepless nights passed by, and I decided to hire private investigators. They searched through her room without much of a lead as to her whereabouts. There was however one exception- a picture in her closet of a California license plate. They asked for her most recent photo to use for their investigation. That afternoon they spoke with her previous place of employment, teachers at her school, and friends to find out if anyone knew where she might be.

Her friends said that they had no idea where she was. All they knew was that she was headed on a trip. I was beginning to feel like this had become a conspiracy behind my back. Upon the investigators questioning, her friends did tell them that Shannon had thrown her cell phone into the nearby harbor. Realizing this, my heart skipped a beat because I knew that I had no way of contacting her.

I decided to track all her outgoing cell phone calls in the last month. I found a toll-free phone number in our last month's statement, and knew it was a lead. She was meticulous about not leaving any traces behind her except for this one phone call, which led me to Amtrak. I spoke with Amtrak service, and they apologetically said they couldn't give me any information because she was at the legal age of eighteen. She was considered an adult, excluding me from any further information. The next day, I finally received confirmation from the local police department. They informed me that she took Amtrak from New York to Chicago. From there she went across the rest of the country and finally arrived in Los Angeles, California. I pictured her spending days on this runaway train from the life that she once lived, far away from all the people that loved her the most. I just couldn't seem to understand why she left this way.

Every hour that went by, I waited in hope for her to contact me. Five agonizing days later, I received her first contact via email. She didn't give any details of where she was or why she left; only that she was on an adventure meeting new people and seeing new places. She refused to give me any details, fearing that I would find her and force her to come back home. I didn't mention to her that I was in contact with our local police department and was notified of her general whereabouts; for fear that she would only run even farther.

Later, in the continued investigation, one of Shannon's friends finally spoke up, stating that they went into New York City with her the day she left home. They confessed they had lunch with her and saw her off on the Amtrak train. These were the very same girls that previously were questioned by the investigators, swearing they knew nothing at all.

Suddenly, they seemed to know a lot more than they originally stated. They not only waved Shannon goodbye, but they drove her car back from the train station to the school parking lot for me to find later. Her brand-new car was sitting two blocks from my house in the vacant parking lot of the school's property. I had no idea how it wasn't towed away, vandalized, or stolen.

After her first email was received, we were without any further contact. I was left completely in the dark. I had no idea where she was, or exactly why she ran away. Her friends covered up the truth for her as she made her way across the country and into these unknown places. None of these people seemed to consider her safety or my sanity. I felt outsmarted by her deceptive lies and left in the dark with virtually nothing.

She spent an entire year prior to the runaway saving all her money as a waitress. She saved every penny of it, and yet I never asked her what she was saving it for. We allowed her to save her own money, without ever asking her to pay for anything. We loved her, fed her, bought her clothes, kept a roof over her head, and anything else she needed we paid for including a brand-new car for her 18th birthday. I was heartbroken that while she planned this runaway behind our backs, she willingly accepted everything we did for her as if it meant nothing at all. I couldn't even allow myself to be angry with her because I was overwhelmed with the guilt of being unable to fulfill my role as her mother.

Before she left home, she closed the savings account that we originally started for her and transferred this money into her own private bank account. I didn't have any access to this new account to see if there was any activity from her. She wanted to be sure there was no way we could trace where she was going. However, Amtrak required her driver's license as identification to board the train. Thankfully, this was how they traced her location.

It was a clean break from the life she lived and all the people who loved her dearly. She carried this out with extreme measures, spending years researching and premeditating her runaway plan. By this point, the agony I felt from everything that had taken place was emotionally paralyzing. Without any sleep, the days had no end, and the shock of her absence left me completely numb.

For a period, I went through a series of emotions following her disappearance. My first reaction was shock. This was followed by worry, guilt, sheer terror, hurt, anger, disbelief, disappointment, and heartbreak. Each one of these emotions had a multitude of horrifying thoughts and feelings that followed. It sent me straight down into a pit of depression with my emotional despair and dragged on with no end in sight.

I honestly believed that Shannon didn't realize the magnitude of what she had done to our family. However, I knew there would come a day where she would have to face the cold harsh reality of the wounded hearts that she left behind. God revealed to me that the truth would one day come to the surface, and all the reasons for her secret runaway would eventually be uncovered.

Chapter 4

Cover Up

Where was the respect, concern, or compassion for one another, especially amongst the women that knew of my daughter Shannon? It seemed to me that her friends and their families should have been more interested in where she was than hiding the truth from me. Most of her friends knew something about this runaway plan, and yet not one person made the right decision to tell me the truth about it. Instead, they were more concerned with only covering up her secret, to cover for their own part in this lie.

The mother of my daughter's friend wasn't concerned about telling the truth when both her and her daughter knew all about this carefully planned runaway. In fact, after speaking with this mother for the first time, I was left with a feeling that she knew more than what she led me to believe. Consequently, I called her back a few weeks later, only to find she had Shannon's new cell phone number all along. She kept it from me until I was insistent that her daughter must have had it as a contact on her cellphone. Low and behold, when I urged her to search through her daughter's phone multiple times, she suddenly found Shannon's number. I was absolutely appalled that all along they had her new cell phone number, while I was left in complete torment.

After this phone call, I was left with only a scrap piece of paper with her cell phone number. This could have been the very moment I called Shannon and ended this silence between us. For some reason, I just knew that I had to wait for her willingness to call me first. After all, she ran away from me, and only when she was ready to speak to me again would it be the right time. I cannot even describe how tremendously challenging it was not to pick up the phone to reach out to her first. So many times, I picked up my phone and just stared at her number wanting desperately to talk to her again. However, I knew as her mother that I needed to gain her respect and crawling back to her wasn't going to help me get it.

As the situation continued to unfold, I realized this mother and her daughter withheld vital information from me. Her secretive information seemed more important than Shannon's safety. They both were only concerned with keeping their mouths shut and pretending they knew nothing at all. They were more concerned with being sworn to secrecy, than stepping up and telling the truth. Even after they were questioned by the authorities and my desperate plea for help, they made no attempt to tell the truth.

As it states in (Leviticus 5:1), "If you are called to testify about something you have seen or that you know about, it is sinful to refuse to testify, and you will be punished for your sin." They were in no way innocent bystanders as they turned their heads as though they knew nothing.

Was the fear of a lawsuit from being a liability to the situation so great that the truth could not be told? Maybe if the truth was told from the beginning, this tragedy wouldn't have even occurred. These people were liable for being accomplices and negating to tell the truth, even though the opportunity to help me was knocking at their door.

I was completely outraged that from one mother to another, there was no compassion for my desperation to find my daughter. There aren't enough words to explain the anguish I felt, not knowing where Shannon was during this time, and then finding out later that so many knew of her plans, and yet denied me of this information. It was undeniably one big conspiracy behind my back. It snowballed out of control and into a tragedy that could have easily been avoided. Nevertheless, I eventually learned to find a way through the Word of God to have mercy on them all for their ignorant behavior.

I am in no way excusing Shannon's actions, or her friend's accountability for keeping this runaway secret from me. I know there had to be a feeling of loyalty amongst her friends, being sworn into secrecy. But then again, someone should have had the sense to tell the truth for the sake of her safety alone. It would have only taken one person to make a stand for what was right. Shannon wasn't taking a trip around the corner; she was headed for the opposite end of the country all by herself! This was a lost girl, and my crises were complicated by people who knowingly withheld the truth.

The lack of concern for one another, and how society displayed itself throughout this event, showed me just how ignorant we really are without wisdom. Furthermore, the ultimate example of these low standards was in their willingness to support Shannon's behavior, by keeping a defiant secret. They were all a part of this conspiracy due to the hidden secret, and knowingly went along with it behind my back.

During the time of my distress, there was not one person, other than my immediate family members, willing to help me. I felt completely alone in my struggles to find her. I spent months with my family's concerns but was without any answers for what I was going through. I felt alone, and could barely get off the couch, as I suffered with severe depression for months. The only way I was able to keep my head above water was by praying and believing in the promises of God's Word.

It seemed that most people's only interest was to ask me to prying questions and give me nothing more than their heartless opinions. Very few people asked me how I was doing, or if they could do anything to support me during this difficult time. This was just the saddest case of people's self-centered behavior that I have ever witnessed. In times of trouble, I was left alone without any support, in a town full of people that personally knew my daughter.

Nevertheless, no matter how bleak things may have seemed, I had hope and belief in my prayers. I didn't allow any of my given circumstances to discourage my faith, knowing that

24

Shannon would be safe. During everything that was falling apart, my faith was all I had to pull me through this unforeseen time of struggle.

Chapter 5

A Glimpse of Vision

The only lead I had to find Shannon was to contact my friend John, whose friendship I made in recent months. He was a friend of Mike and former bodybuilding training partner, but he had lost contact with John when he moved to Los Angeles over two decades ago.

Unbeknownst to my husband, his secretary also knew of John's family years prior to Shannon's disappearance. He decided to rekindle their friendship by asking his secretary if John's family would forward his email to him. He reached John by email, and they began speaking regularly on the phone thereafter. Mike had shared with me that John was a very inspiring person, and that he had become a devoted Christian since they had spoken years prior.

He asked me to call John on a few occasions, so that I could have the opportunity to hear about his inspirational beliefs. This was before Shannon's disappearance, and I had absolutely no plans of making that phone call to him. The last thing I wanted to do at that point in my life was to have someone preach to me about God, but for some reason John persistently asked for me to contact him. I believed that he wanted to reach out to me and share about the greatness in his life since his relationship with the Lord. He probably gathered from previous conversations with my husband, that I was lost.

Miraculously, as the year went on, I began seeking God. I came across many Christian books and slowly began realizing that spirituality was indeed a weakness in my life. These inspiring books gave me practical advice for solving problems in my own life through God's great wisdom. I continued to follow various Christian ministries and had a vision of what it would be like to have my own one day. I can recall giving up this dream inside of my heart thinking that it seemed so far out of reach. I couldn't seem to find my faith and thought the opportunity to have a ministry was just a dream that I'd never have. So, instead of living my life based on my true heart's desire for having my own ministry, I made the decision to take a course to become a personal trainer. Talk about taking a left turn in life, this was certainly it for me. Although, it was a challenge for me because I hadn't any type of education since high school. I seemed to enjoy the challenge of learning something entirely new in my life. I had been weight training for the past couple of years and enjoyed working out and keeping healthy and fit. With a personal interest in this field, I pursued any avenue to continually learn about it.

My connection to speaking with Mike's friend John finally came about when he came to me one day and said, "My friend John is a professional bodybuilder and personal trainer. He would be happy to teach you anything you want to know about personal training." I thought about it and decided I would call him. I felt a bit awkward because this was completely out of character for me. I was not the type of person to just call a stranger and ask for their advice. Yet, for some very strange reason, I decided to call him anyway.

Initially, we began our conversation speaking about the details of personal training. This was followed by John sharing with me his life's success and God being the center of it all. He shared his story about how God had come into his life with a near death experience, and he began studying the Bible from that point forward. He spoke so eloquently about it, that it made me feel God's greater presence right then and there.

During our second phone call, I expressed to John that it was no longer my desire to speak about personal training anymore with him. I decided that I was more in need of a Christian spiritual coach. This came to me after our first conversation when I prayed for the first time seriously to God about what I needed in my life. This was absolutely the prayer that would begin to change everything. I never heard anything about spiritual coaching prior to my prayer, but for some reason this is what was placed in my heart. I had this feeling that God had planned this precisely, as a way of fulfilling His plans for me.

John suggested that I begin by reading the Bible every day. I bought an amplified Bible and started reading it right away. John and I spoke monthly while he continued to teach me about the Word of God. He mentioned a friend of his named Sammy, who had a Christian ministry and told me to begin following him on his Facebook page for daily spiritual nuggets. John told me that he was going to start me off with spiritual guidance, and eventually would let his friend take over to help me. It struck me quite strangely as to why I wouldn't work with Sammy right away. Nevertheless, I didn't question it and continued with John's guidance instead.

Around this time, my mother was diagnosed with cancer. God became a bigger part in my life because my faith helped me through this terrible time. I had gained some knowledge of the Word of God by this point and shared my faith with her as well. It took one long, stressful, and very miserable year for my mother's treatments to be completed. We prayed for her healing, and she has been cancer-free ever since, despite the poor prognosis of stage four cancer from her doctor!

After the first few days of Shannon's disappearance, I debated about whether I should send John a picture of her as my only source of somehow finding her being that he lived in Los Angeles. I was hopeful he might by some small chance see her. I decided that no matter how small the odds were that he could somehow find her, it was worth trying.

Although he didn't recognize her by the picture, he told his friend Sammy about the situation. Sammy also lived in Los Angeles. Within only a couple of days, I was surprised and excited to hear a message on my phone from Sammy, and his desire to help guide me through his mentoring. I thought back to that moment when John said he would help give me some guidance, until his friend would step in to do so. I thought to myself, "WOW, this was obviously about perfect timing!"

When I learned what Sammy did through his ministry, I realized that he was a very special man. He fed the homeless and mentored anyone in need of life changes. I took one look at him on his website, and I knew he was someone extraordinary. Instantly, I was intrigued by his website pictures that showed how he lived his life by giving to the needs of others. I could see from his pictures the genuine love that he had to offer. The display of his love for these people was above and beyond anything I had ever noticed before. I was touched that a stranger would have such a loving heart, and that he reached out to help me from three thousand miles across the country. I never dreamed someone as special as Sammy would come into my life and care about me.

In the years prior to knowing Sammy, I thought that God spoke to my heart on a few occasions. One day, I had an inner vision that someone new was going to come into my life. I can remember when I first received this message, I looked around as if to say, "where is this person?" A soft whisper answered me instantly and said, "You don't have to look for him, he will find you." I didn't have any idea exactly what this meant. For the first time in my entire life, I wondered if I heard a message from God.

This message was so clear to me that to this day, I can remember exactly where I was when I heard it. I can recall it so vividly in my mind, as I shopped in the produce aisle of the supermarket looking through my grocery list. I remember placing zucchinis in a bag, and out of nowhere I heard a voice reveal this message to me. Since then, there were times in my life when I came across a new person and questioned if they were the one sent according to this message, but realized somewhere deep within, it wasn't the one I thought God told me about. I knew someone was out there somewhere and would one day fulfill this message that I heard.

Somewhere along the mentoring process with Sammy, it suddenly hit me. I thought that he may somehow have been the connection to the message that was given to me. It seemed to me that he was not only the person that was supposed to come into my life to help me, but his ministry could have been the missing piece of the puzzle that could allow me the experience of ministering to people myself.

I can remember for some unknown reason feeling shear excitement when I spoke to Sammy in our very first conversation. I knew I was missing something in my life, but honestly, I didn't realize it until I spoke with him. It seemed odd that even after enduring the heartbreaking news of Shannon's runaway, his voice seemed to light a spark somewhere deep inside of me. I felt a sense of hope for the first time in years.

I can remember the first embarrassing thing I blurted out to him was that I felt like I was speaking to a famous movie star, but this was the only way I could explain how I felt. I was aware that he was a Hollywood stuntman, but his fame with me felt very different. I'm still not exactly sure how to explain it, other than I felt there was going to be something more to this than what meets the eye, and the meaning of this relationship, than what I knew of at the time. I just knew at this point, God gave me the feeling that Sammy was going to play a significant part in my life, and Shannon's as well.

He began our conversation by sharing about his wisdom and his dealings with many runaways. I thought to myself, "What was the likelihood of having just the right person help me, regardless of the thousands of miles between us, and help bring Shannon to safety?" This more than made up for the previous lack of help in my hometown.

I hadn't met Sammy in person, and yet during our phone calls together, he literally pulled me through the toughest months of heartache from Shannon's runaway. I was guided through the roughest point of my life, and along the way he taught me how to handle her runaway, and especially how not to make matters any worse.

His top priority was to offer his love and care for anyone who needed help. This always made me forget that he was a Hollywood stuntman. It was his loving heart, not his celebrity status, that most impressed me.

Over the next few months, I received only email contacts from Shannon and vague reasons for her actions. Sammy prayed with me for her safety wherever she was. He said to me during our conversation that I needed to allow her to run until she didn't want to run anymore. I knew that I had to be stronger and more patient than I had ever been to have her back again. Meanwhile, I began working on myself through the mentoring to improve many things in my own life.

We began the mentorship with basic Bible study. I studied the Word of God, but this time I learned how to apply it to my life. I began reading the Bible every day, sometimes all day to get through the pain and the sudden void of Shannon. She was thousands of miles away and I missed her terribly, but I refused to fall apart. I wanted to come out of this a stronger person and have a better relationship with her because of it.

The day she left; God had undoubtedly given me a reassured feeling that I was finally going to rise above the mess in my life. This revelation came to me on the most tragic day of my life, not only as a wakeup call, but as a strength in my weakest moment. From that moment on, I knew something unexplainable changed inside of me forever.

This newfound inner strength was the most powerful life changing moment of my life. My entire life flashed before me like a picture being taken of everything in my past all at once. I knew many areas in my life had gone very wrong for me. However, I knew this was the very beginning of changes that were long overdue, but I still had many things to face and a long road ahead of me.

Chapter 6

The Heart of Forgiveness

I still could not wrap my mind around Shannon running away from home and the pain that I was left with from her betrayal. I hadn't a clue where to even begin to resolve this hurt inside of me, and between the two of us, but God certainly did. I spent all my time seeking Him relentlessly for the answers to mend my broken heart.

Throughout the months however, I found myself dreaming of the moment when I would hear her sweet voice again. Waiting for her return was the most emotionally challenging point of my life. Most nights were sleepless and filled with so much of the unknown. Even so, I worked tirelessly in preparing for the day of our first conversation together. I knew as a mother that I had caused a lot of pain and heartache, and I desperately wanted her to notice the change in me since she ran away from home.

I leaned into God more and more each day to find the strength to heal and was becoming more empowered by the renewal of my mind. I was gaining a different perspective with a new attitude to restore my soul. Even though she had broken my trust in her, I was entrusting God to bring us back together again, and better than before.

The first phase of my emotional healing since the day she left was learning how to truly love her, even though she had hurt me deep to the core. In the past, bitterness and resentment was my go-to as a protective barrier for anyone who tried to hurt me, but this time I wanted to learn how to become free of that behavior to overcome the conflict with righteousness.

As a matter of fact, my own bitter grudges were the deadly poison that had affected all my relationships. Every day was an emotional struggle, as I constantly wrestled with many different scenarios of resentful thoughts about things that hurt me in the past. My heart had hardened, and I was trapped amongst my ill feelings, but was beginning to learn that these feelings were contrary to God's Word. My own negative and critical way of thinking only kept me in a constant state of inner war and put distance between myself and my family.

The wisdom I was gaining from God's Word had the ultimate power to purge these bitter wars out of me. My heart was ever-changing as His promises were washing away my impure thoughts to help heal these wounds. This process led me to understand many problems about the condition of my bitter attitude that I didn't realize I had before. Facing the truth about the consequential problems in my life was helping me to make permanent changes to rebuild my future.

I knew the Holy Spirit couldn't successfully work inside of me while holding onto the anger and bitter grudges related to Shannon's run away. The truth says, "In your anger do not sin. Do not let the sun go down while you are still angry. Do not give the devil a foothold" (Ephesians 4:26).

She had been gone for some time now, and the last thing that I wanted was for Satan to take a foothold and have his way with my soul. I was finally making conscious decisions that would forever change the vicious cycle of my brokenness. I knew that working on strengthening a bitter soul would not create a better outcome in any of my relationships.

This is not to say that I did not acknowledge the hurt and rejection that I felt when she secretly disappeared from our lives. I came to realize however, that if I continued to react to this situation based on my initial feelings, the bitterness would have only festered, and my attempt to forgive her would not have been genuine. Holding a grudge would only have hindered us from changing the hurtful things between us and prevented the relationship from healing.

By this point, I absolutely refused to walk around as a wounded victim. It was time that I placed a higher value on my ever-growing relationship with the Lord for my healing. My new faith-filled hope rose from within me and released me from the bondage that chained me to so much pain. It set me free from the torment of bitter grudges, and the mindset of having to acquire some type of revenge. I was continually reminded of Colossians 1:13," that with forgiveness, we would be rescued from the darkness of this tragedy", and I was eagerly looking forward to that day!

My only intent was to learn how to love her through this process and show mercy on her. I believed wholeheartedly that God would be the one to open her heart to receive truth about her tragic decision to run away from home. This process covered all bases for me to be able to move forward with the confident expectancy of her return. As my heart filled with the kind of hope and peace that was unlike anything I had ever experienced before, I could not deny the incredible power of the Holy Spirit at work inside of me. All at once, I seemed to notice the overwhelming pain had vanished from my heart and was replaced with an indescribable joy that was apparent to others in such a time of distress. This kind of hope kept me from seeking any type of revenge and gave me an ability to have an unconditional love for her.

Ever since she ran away from home, I couldn't help but notice that I had this inner feeling I still may have had some of my own sins that I hadn't fully faced and realized I would eventually have to apologize for the extensive damage that I had caused her too. I knew deep down that I had no business pointing fingers at her, until I found myself blameless for this mess that I was standing in right along with her.

Matthew 7:1-2 sheds light on hypocritical judgement by saying, "Do not judge, or you too will be judged. For the same way you judge others, you will be judged, and with the measure you use, it will be measured to you."

I knew in my heart that I had plenty of work left to do on myself before I could ever judge her fairly for what she had done. I couldn't help but think of the verse in John 8:7 when Jesus said, "He that is without sin among you, let him first cast a stone at her" and suddenly realized my own conviction of sin would not allow me to judge anyone else's behavior with a clear conscience.

While my feelings were deeply offended and the wounds were still painfully raw, I made the choice to work through the bitterness and anger by doing things God's way. The cause of my internal struggle was in the cold harsh reality of feeling utterly rejected, and of being a failure as a mother. I knew that only God could heal these wounds by delivering me from my own guilt-ridden sins and fill my heart with His eternal love. I realized that only my repentance would release me of the guilt from my past and failing to do the things that I knew I should have done as a mother. It was time to start confessing all my sins to start anew and put the past behind me.

Although there was a period when all I could think about was how Shannon mistreated me, I realized that I had more to gain by being hopeful that there would be a chance of forgiveness and reconciliation between us. I also knew that if I didn't take these first steps of faith to purify my heart and mind that I'd never be able to offer her my forgiveness when she was ready to apologize to me. The conflict would have only lingered inside of me and damaged the future of our relationship. The benefits of being faithful were in the hopes of having that moment of forgiveness and reconciling our differences. The kind of hope that our future held far outweighed holding any type of grudge.

Although I believed that she had to be somewhat aware that she was doing something wrong by running away, I also knew that she was unaware of the spirit in her which caused her to do it. At this point in her life, she did not make the right choices because she was unaware of the power of deception. She was virtually overtaken by the spirit of the enemy's lies and convinced herself that she didn't have any other choice than to chase her dreams by running away from home. She had most certainly become the prodigal daughter, but what was far worse was realizing that she was tragically following in my own footsteps. She had learned to run away from her problems and abandon the ones she was to love the most.

I had come to understand that the tragedy of her runaway was not a struggle against flesh and blood, but the power of this dark world and against spiritual forces in the heavenly realms, as revealed in Ephesians 6:12. In other words, I knew that I had to hate the sin, but learn to love the sinner that was held captive by the snare of her sin. Separating the two was another aspect that helped me to heal, knowing deep in my heart that her sin wasn't really who she was deep down inside. I cannot adequately explain how the power of healing behind these perspectives freed my soul from such deep anguish.

Shannon was bound to rebel without the Holy Spirit guiding her life, just as I once was. I've come to realize that it is not only knowing what God commands of us that is essential but obeying Him as well. As it says in 1 John 2:3- 4, "We know that we have come to know Him if we keep His commands. Whoever says I know Him but does not know what He commands is a liar, and the truth is not in that person." A person who continues to avoid the truth will be a runner for the rest of their lives. Everything they do is bred from sin and built on a foundation of quicksand. Inevitably, the more they struggle with denying their sins, the deeper they will sink into a life of tragedy and despair. Sadly, this was truly the picture of what our lives had become.

The so called "healing process" in the previous years of my life, had only allowed time to accumulate years of bitterness and resentment that negatively impacted my marriage. There was never any solid communication or an understanding of one another's genuine feelings. Quite honestly, at that time, I really had no way to decipher the truth about what I was genuinely feeling anyway. My mind was only filled with a state of utter chaos and confusion.

Over the decades of our marriage, the level of unresolved hurt standing between Mike and I had built solid walls between us. Trying to climb over these protective walls to regain intimacy seemed like an impossible hurtle. Over the years, the walls were only built higher and higher, and the chance for true intimacy seemed to become non-existent. There were hardly ever any signs of humility from either one of us to be able to offer an apology and resolve our conflicts.

We were only left surrounded by the pain of our own unwillingness to change and start anew.

During this process, I began to understand the depths of God's Word about love and forgiveness. I knew that I was discovering entirely new perspectives for all my relationships to begin healing. I found myself taking the proper steps of faith to restore my personal relationships. I knew that once a genuine and heart filled form of repentance took place in our family that forgiveness should be given freely. Only then would we have a true reconciling of our relationships because sin would no longer separate us.

Chapter 7

To Hear Her Voice Again

By this time, the cold November chill was in the air with the sure signs of winter just around the corner. The months slowly crept by, and the holidays were soon approaching. We were once a family that thrived on the holiday spirit and our togetherness. However, with the situation being what it was, I knew the holidays had to go on regardless of Shannon not being home. Nevertheless, my heart still felt joy from my faith, as things were evidently changing within my own life.

It was the week before Thanksgiving, and any glimmer of hope of Shannon coming back home for the holidays was beginning to fade. So, I focused on the rest of my family and spending the holidays together. Her absence was not going to stop me from living my life anymore. I was confident with my hope in God that this nightmare would soon be resolved.

Late one afternoon, while I was preparing dinner, my cellphone rang unexpectedly. I glanced over at it and paused for a second, realizing it was Shannon's name that appeared on the screen. By this time, there were months of silence between us. I knew this was finally the moment that would change everything. I stared at the phone for a moment and couldn't believe I was finally going to hear her sweet voice again.

Every moment of missing her over the last three months had led up to this point. Although I was nervous to finally speak with her, I answered the phone as if it were just an ordinary day. Although, by this point, I hadn't any idea what ordinary really was anymore.

As I put the phone closer to my ear, I heard her say, "Hi Mom" and it was truly a surreal moment. Months had passed without one word from her, but by the tone of her voice, it sounded as if we had never skipped a beat. I was finally able to see the light at the end of this dark tunnel. Overcome with such emotion, I was practically speechless for the right thing to say to her.

As my emotions quickly swung around, I thought back to when we used to talk to each other on a regular basis. It was beyond my worst nightmare to suddenly endure not knowing when I would ever hear from her again. I realized at that very moment what a gift it was just to be able to pick up the phone and say, "I love you." I knew instantly that I would never take it for granted again.

As I heard the first words spring from my lips, there was suddenly a moment of silence. I said, "Hello Shannon" and everything went silent between us. She waited to hear what I had to say next. She was completely unaware of the love in my heart, until I spoke out with the sheer joy of finally hearing from her. I don't know how, but I put everything standing between us aside, to have this conversation be one that we would always remember had changed everything. I could hear in her voice that she was taken back by the calm

43

and loving sound of my voice. I knew she was expecting me to give her a piece of my mind, but truthfully, the only thought that was on my mind at this point was THANKING GOD, she finally called me!

As we tried to continue our conversation however, awkward silence was between us. I spoke with her searching desperately for something that would create a connection, but this was not one of those conversations where it just clicked, like, "You had me at hello." After our first words, it seemed I was speaking to a stranger on the other end of a long-distance call. Fear struck me because I never wanted to be faced with losing her again. Saying the wrong thing was not on my list with this uncertain possibility.

I knew by the tone in her voice that it was obvious she felt guilt ridden by what she had done. I certainly was not going to add to it or condemn her for it. She needed my support if I was ever to be included in her life again. It was up to me to take the first step to show her my love. To be clear on this, I did not support her decision to run away, but I was willing to let former things go at this time, for the promise of a new beginning between us. I wanted to support her dreams and desires, which I had failed to do in the past.

None of what I was saying however, seemed to be penetrating through the solid walls, which she had built around herself. I was becoming progressively more nervous that I hadn't the right words to gain a connection between us. Suddenly, I heard a voice deep within my heart urging me to say, "No matter what your reason was for running

44

away, I never lost faith in God, and that things would change between us." "I love you no matter what circumstances ever come our way."

Immediately, the dullness from her voice was lifted and gave way for the sound of enthusiasm. With a profound excitement in her voice she said, "This was exactly what I wanted to hear you say to me Mom!" I was completely relieved that I had finally found heartfelt words to say to her. It was my unconditional love for her that she desired.

Those very loving words that managed to rise from my heart had been long buried underneath all of what had happened. During this conversation however, I felt the strong presence of God standing amongst the two of us. I prayed that God would give me the right words to say because honestly, I hadn't a clue.

No words could ever explain the change that happened between us in that heartfelt moment, other than knowing it was supernatural. I knew if I didn't say what she needed to hear from me in that very moment, it would have closed the windows to her heart all over again. Afterwards, she said "Mom, the change I hear in you changes everything for me." Although it seemed there was a sudden change in a matter of seconds, it took months to prepare my heart for the right words to come out of my mouth.

By this point, I wanted nothing more but for her to share her dreams with me. I knew that if I didn't run alongside of her, she would feel as though I were plotting against her. It was important for me to be on her side, and I was willing to do whatever it took to get there. Although it was a poor decision for her to run away, I was still responsible for not supporting her dreams and desires in the past. I was way too busy trying to control the outcome of her future for my benefit.

Having God ever-present during our conversation was precisely what we both needed. This was a new beginning for both of us to be able to restore the brokenness between us. God had changed my heart in ways that helped me rejuvenate not only myself, but to begin to restore my relationship with her as well.

For so long our relationship was strained by the fact that her trust for me was compromised. There were many things that I did which contributed to our demise. The noticeably dissatisfying life that I was living was not a feeling of stability for her over the years. It seemed however, that my newfound relationship with God finally allowed for her to find this feeling of trust for me. In the past, there wasn't ever an understanding between the two of us. She just kept her deepest and most intimate desires hidden away from me.

In all her years prior to this incident, she managed to hide the secretive plans for her life, and strategically gained my trust, so that I would never suspect anything out of the ordinary. Unfortunately, her leaving in the way she had nearly destroyed us completely. The despair from the unexpected course of events seemed impossible to rise above. The torment I faced as I repeatedly battered and blamed myself for this disaster was a daily war zone inside of me. However, I knew it was too soon to question her reasons for running away to have any kind of truthful answers from her standpoint.

As a mother, it took a tremendous amount of self-restraint to keep my mouth shut. No one else in my family seemed to understand just how important it was for me to follow the leading of the Holy Spirit. I knew the fragile state of our relationship could only be restored by trusting in God. I was certain of the path He laid out before me, and none of the circumstances I faced moved me. God's timing was essential, and I needed not to rush ahead of Him.

As our first conversation ended, I felt my heart begin to sink. I didn't want to say goodbye to her ever again. After the long months of her awaited call, the conversation ended in a quick moment of time. She must have heard the sudden sadness in my voice and reassured me that she would be calling me again very soon. She gave me a sense of hope that she wanted to be in my life again, and God knew this was exactly what I needed to hear from her too.

Saying goodbye was inexpressibly a heart wrenching moment. Not knowing when I would hear from her again, or where she was even living, took my complete trust in God. I looked to Him for her safety and knew things were changing. After finally saying goodbye, I couldn't deny feeling completely estranged from her once again. Yet, despite the distance that set us apart, it was undeniably God who would bring us back together again.

Chapter 8

Worldly Deceptions

I couldn't keep myself from reading the cold-hearted letter she left behind on that dreadful day. I kept searching for the unanswered mysteries of her words. As I examined every sentence she wrote, I tried to understand her reasons for running away. I never found any comfort in the uncertainty of her words. God's Word made it obvious to me that she was not at all living in God's will and trying to understand her decisions for leaving would be completely absurd.

I honestly believed she was blinded by a glorified dream, which she had vaguely mentioned in her letter. She didn't state exactly what her dream was that she so greatly desired. Nevertheless, it forced her to end our togetherness as a family. This dream had become her idol, and betrayal was the result. I believe the importance of her dream took precedence at a time when she needed me the most. Unfortunately, at that time in my life, I was predisposed in the depths of my own despair and was in no condition to be of support to anyone.

The years of my life passed by with a feeling of emotional disconnect from everyone. This unfortunately caused her to turn elsewhere for the answers she needed in her life. The persuasions from the outside world impacted her life greatly with nothing but deception. The cultivation of her friends, television, and music became the ultimate source of her influence. The worldly persuasions were the impetus to the downfall to her life in so many ways.

The kind of music she listened to filled her with a belief system and whispered lies that led her astray. She identified with the words of pop music day in and day out. After she left home, I found the music CD's she had been listening to over the years. I realized this music had filled her head with all kinds of negative emotions, as she tried to discover and identify herself through the destructive words. I remember how terrified I was when I began listening to this dark music. I honestly believed that she felt she was more understood by the music, and found a connection to it, rather than to her own mother. Allowing her to listen to this kind of music only fed the fire, and eventually it burned completely out of control.

The outside influences were strong enough to persuade her against her own family. The feelings in the songs only magnified her emotions by feeding her mind with improper thoughts every day. The tiny buds were constantly plugged into her ear drums, so she couldn't miss a beat. She slowly drifted away, as the noise drowned us out of her life, and the swirling sound of music became her God.

She became fascinated with Hollywood pop stars and fame. The walls in her room were adorned with posters of her favorite singers. She knew I did not approve of some of them. However, I never put my foot down by forbidding her to listen to them either. It was only in hindsight that I realized the magnitude of havoc it managed to cause in all our lives. I felt strongly that her unfortunate decision to leave was influenced by this evil dark music.

She identified with the words in the music, as if it held the unequivocal answers as to how she should live her life. I know the evil persuasion took over her life and encouraged her to run away. Her motivation came from a place that she didn't even realize herself, and it all stemmed from something as seemingly innocent as the words in pop music and was glorified in her mind.

She was innocently unaware of her idol's influence and made a devastating mistake in the way she was going about attaining her dreams. The inundations from earthly standards in pop culture diluted her decisions to have a proper perspective. This belief system lured her into sinful decisions, which were based on the negative words in the songs and the emotions behind them. Music becomes one of the most important influences for most teenagers. It usually is at the most vulnerable changing point in their lives from childhood to adulthood.

It seemed like "the norm" to just let her go along with the influence of this pop music because every other kid was also listening to it too. When I look back, it seemed as though I were more concerned with her fitting in with the crowd than doing what was right. Unfortunately, it took the tragic incident of Shannon's runaway before I became aware of the steep price I would have to pay. It's unfortunate that I was unaware of the power of words at that time. I subsequently learned that they can be a blessing or a curse in our lives.

It says in Ephesians 4:29, "Let no foul or polluted language, nor evil word nor unwholesome talk come out of your mouth, but in such speech as is good and beneficial to spiritual progress of others, as fitting to the need and the occasion, that it may be a blessing and give grace to those who hear it." Proverbs 18:21 says "The tongue has the power of life and death, and those who love it will eat its fruits."

I only wished that I had this wisdom long ago to understand that the impact of negative words can create actions that are evil. The words she repeatedly rehearsed were swirling around in her mind, and eventually they gave way for what she believed in her heart.

During this time of her life, I also noticed she kept her thoughts and feelings hidden away inside of her amongst her songs. It seemed as if I was just an outsider, and on some days, I felt like her enemy. I thought this was just the typical kind of behavior for a teenager. I never once thought she was capable of skillfully planning this entire scheme of events behind our back.

I had trusted her explicitly since she never gave me a single day of trouble in her entire life. It was foolish of me to have thought that I always knew where she was and what she was doing. She never once broke her curfew, which was substantially earlier than all her friends. I mistakenly believed I had it all under control, but only when I fooled

51

myself that I knew how to raise my kids the right way. I suddenly realized that I was completely deluded believing I was ever in total control of her every move.

Considering Shannon's integrity, I was blindsided by her doing something this dreadful to us as a family. It was so out of character for her, which made her runaway more shocking. I didn't even know who my own daughter was anymore, or ever did for that matter. All at once, I felt our entire relationship seemed like a farce to me.

I realized that my role as a mother, and the discernment that was greatly needed, was lacking without God. She had become completely vulnerable and misled into the world's temptations. I was reminded of this harsh reality by the suffering of our consequences since her runaway.

As I thought back, trying to put all the pieces of our lives back together again, I remembered that she briefly mentioned her desire to attend college in California. I strongly objected to this idea and refused to even consider it at this time. In my better judgement, I thought it was too far from home, and that she needed to choose a college more nearby. If she were that serious about going, we could have considered other options, after she had proven that attending college to get a degree was truly her goal. In my mind, going to California wasn't open for discussion otherwise. In her mind however, she was determined to go one way or another. When I look back, I had to give myself some credit. It was because of that good ole mother's intuition that I knew something was fishy, and she was just testing the waters to see if we would be on board with her living in California. Since it seemed that I was not, she justified having to run away from home to accomplish her dreams.

Honestly, I knew that she did not have an honest desire to attend college at that point in time. I had a gut feeling that she wanted to go to California with other motives in mind, but I never dreamed it was to run away from home. I finally let go of the subject, but because I lacked the discernment necessary to fully understand that she was up to no good, it left the door wide open for her to disappear from our lives. I was hoping her desire to go to California was just a passing phase for her, but I was so very, very wrong.

During the months leading up to her runaway, I also thought to myself that Shannon was not the type of person to just sit around after she graduated from high school. Meanwhile, she didn't seem to have any other plans, which struck me as quite odd. Looking back, I can recall thinking, "When is she going to finally drop the bomb about what she really wants to do with her life." I knew there was something she was hiding, and she just wasn't being honest.

Her dream to live in California was certainly not at all what I envisioned for her life. As her mother, I thought I knew what was best for her future and tried to control her life's outcome. While Mike and I were raising our children, our perspective as parents was skewed. We were mistaken within our own belief system too and were certain that we had the sole right to plan for her future. I believed on the sole basis of giving birth to my daughter that I was entitled to give birth to all her dreams as well.

I based my parenting on the preconceived notion that I knew what was best for her future. I wondered why I never once asked myself how this was possible, when I failed to know what God's best was for my own future. I held onto the convoluted ideas of the world's mistaken concepts for happiness and fulfillment. I discovered that the world's concepts of happiness had the wrong objectives in mind for creating a divine purpose for anyone. Although we believed in God as a family, we didn't know about the promises in God's Word, or how to live according to His principles for most of our marriage. It seems obvious to me that the so called "Typical Teenage Rebellion" would most likely have been avoided if we had God first and foremost in our lives.

As it says in Proverbs 22:25, "The rod and reproof give wisdom, but a child left to himself brings shame to his mother." I thought back over our lives, knowing then if we had God's wisdom that this entire mess, we found ourselves in, would more than likely not have even existed.

Encouraging her to discover her own God-given strengths should have been done at an early age. We were consumed with forcing the world's ideas upon her, instead of encouraging her to explore her own God-given abilities. I became greatly aware that our persuasion of worldliness had stolen what God truly wanted for all of us. Our way of parenting fell short, as we merely tried to navigate our way without a proper course for her life's direction.

"Take to heart all the words by which I am warning you today, that you may command them to your children, that they may be careful to do all the words of this law. For it is no empty word for you, but your very life…" - Deuteronomy 32:46.

Chapter 9

Stay-At-Home Mother

So far, I have only written about many of my shortcomings as a mother. However, I don't want to sell myself short in all the things that I was for my family. To paint a picture that I was morbidly depressed and completely negligent of my family's needs would not be accurate. My family was no more dysfunctional than the average family trying to survive life's obstacles.

As far back as I can remember, the most prevalent desire in my life was to be a wife and a mother. I had traditional, old-fashioned beliefs that my husband would be the provider, and I would take the role of being a stay-at-home mother. As a child, I had a stay-at-home mother myself, and I can remember that alone providing a form of safety for me. I didn't have to worry about being left on my own or left for the responsibility of some stranger to raise me as a child.

The modern way that other families lived never seemed to make any sense to me. Most children were being raised by everyone else, apart from their own parents. The definition of parenting is "the raising of a child by its parents" (Merriam-Webster.com). Women, naturally being more nurturing than men, are made to be the primary caretakers of their own children. It says in Deuteronomy 6:6-7, "We are

56

supposed to be available to them morning, noon and night."
I believed that nurturing children should be a full-time role
which should be taken very seriously. Tending to, caring for,
and supporting their every need took my full-time love and
attention. To my surprise, I learned that I was doing
something right because the Word of God states that we are
"to be self-controlled, pure, working at home, kind, and
submissive to our own husbands, that the Word of God may
not be reviled" (Titus 2:5). The verses have already laid out
the role necessary for a woman to provide the needs of her
family. The stability needed in a family would not be
successfully accomplished without the role of each parent,
which is made very clear according to the Word of God.
Being a keeper at home entails managing a home in an
orderly and loving environment daily. Without ever
knowing the wisdom of God, I innately knew this was the
only way that made sense to raise a family.

Mothering with a full-time career outside the home seemed
nearly impossible to me without it all fraying at the edges.
Dysfunction is defined as "failure to achieve or sustain a
behavioral norm or expected condition, as in a relationship"
(thefreedictionary.com). Is it normal that children spend
their most important years without their mother being the
most significant role model and primary caretaker? As for
myself, this was a no-brainer to figure out.

Looking back, Mike and I had to make MANY financial
sacrifices to make it possible for me to be a stay-at-home
mother. I was not about to hire someone else to raise my

children. I didn't believe it was possible that they would get the love and attention they needed from hired help, or that a grandparent could live up to the exhausting and demanding role of a younger woman.

Although I was struggling as a wife and mother, I was able to achieve certain things, such as strategically planning out a budgeted amount each week to cook my family healthy meals from scratch. I woke up early every morning and made sure my children had a healthy breakfast. I dressed them properly and dropped them off at the front door of their school every day. While they were in school, I cleaned the house, worked out, and ran my husband's business, all of which was in our home. I was suddenly realizing that I was not such a loser after all, and just because Shannon ran away from home, it did not mean that I wasn't doing the best I could at the time.

Today, women have come so far from doing anything that involves being domestic. I had a woman ask me if I knew of a handyman that could change doorknobs and light bulbs in their house. This is a mother who works all week long so she can afford to pay someone else to do something as simple as changing light bulbs and doorknobs. Doesn't this way of thinking cost time away from our children? How many more excuses can be made by not taking the proper accountability for our homes and children? It is my belief that our personal responsibilities should not be delegated to someone else as a substitution for raising children.

These kinds of parents are deceived, thinking they must pay someone else to do what each one of them could be doing themselves. How does a household run properly when the so-called homeowner isn't willing to own up to it? I realized that earning more money to pay for things that were not necessary would have only left my children at home without me.

Over the years, I witnessed a large majority of mothers who ran off to work and left their sick children in school to infect mine. I watched them in disbelief, as they frantically tried to keep up their end of the bargain. Many of their households were falling apart, and so were they. Some of them didn't have the time to feed their family properly, and in effect caused an unhealthy way of living.

Most of these mothers were stressed out, exhausted, disgusted, and irritable. It was as plain as day that they were worn out trying to "do it all". The necessary provisions for raising a family seemed halfhearted and everyone suffered because of it. Raising children is hard enough on its own. Ask any full-time mother just how tough all the years really are. It isn't easy, and many of the days feel personally unfulfilling and frustrating. However, while going off to work may seem like the easy way out, it has a much higher price to pay in the long run.

I could not bear it if my child grew up and realized that someone else had raised them when all they ever really wanted was me. It simply would not live up to the full-time love that was really needed. I often wondered if the motives

59

behind how some mothers lived were truly about loving their children, or were they more about keeping up with the Jones' and the material ways of the world?

I witnessed many families falling apart at the seams, without having the full-time responsibility of a mother being home. God gave us the gift as mothers to bear children and raise them. I believe that it is our responsibility to honor these gifts given to us with our full-time attention.

I dreamed of having extra money, a beautiful home, nice cars, and vacations too. Who doesn't? It took time, effort, self-control, and sacrifice to finally have them. I was never willing, however, to sacrifice my kids to have any of these things. It is God's will that our single most important responsibility (other than a husband) is to raise our own children (and not use hired help or grandparents).

What good is the façade of having a new car, a beautiful house, and vacations, if you have nothing left to give at the end of the day to your personal relationships? It clearly reassures us in Hebrews 13:5, to "Let your character or moral disposition be free from love of money (including greed, avarice, lust, and craving for earthly possessions) and be satisfied with your present (circumstances and with what you have); for He (God) Himself has said, I will not in any way fail you nor give you up nor leave you without support."

You may be asking yourselves by now what good fruits came from me being a Stay-At-Home Mother? After all, Shannon's runaway wasn't a great outcome. Over the months, God gave me the reasons as to why she ran away, and where I went wrong as her mother. However, after gaining much wisdom from the Bible, God showed me that staying at home to raise her was absolutely the right thing to do.

As I studied the Bible, God revealed that because I fulfilled this important role as a mother, and have acknowledged it, I had His favor. As it says in Proverbs 22:6, "Train up a child in the way he should go, and when he is old, he will not depart from it." I had faith that even though she ran away from home, God would eventually reveal to her everything I did right as her mother. It was only a matter of having sheer patience, knowing one day the truth would pour into her heart. One day she would realize just how much I dedicated my life to raising her to the best of my abilities.

Although she was still thousands of miles away and nowhere to be found, I knew in my heart she would return one day. I knew the ties that once bonded us together were too strong to ever be broken. While I may not have been entirely fulfilled within my own life, the fulfillment of knowing who we were as a family was something we could not deny. The amount of love that I managed to provide as her mother would prevail over any evil that stood in our way.

Chapter 10

Memory Lane

Our warmest memories as a family were shared together with the simplistic enjoyment of each other's company. We enjoyed hiking, fishing, biking, and sunsets at the beach. Special occasions were always honored with a time of togetherness and old-fashioned celebration. Most importantly, our everyday life was united with home cooked dinners, and the opportunity to share about the day's events.

Over the years, the recollections of our family vacations left us all with vivid memories. In the summertime, we enjoyed camping in the woods with the simplicity of nature at its best. Most mornings were greeted with the warmth of a sunrise and the sweet scent of fresh morning dew. As the evening fell upon us, we cooked dinner over the warmth of the crackling fire. My kids especially learned the value of being a family on these special occasions, without any of the usual worldly distractions.

They enjoyed collecting sticks as kindling for the nightly campfires with great anticipation for toasted marshmallows. The kids and I romped freely amongst the trees, and relaxation was the name of the game. Camping seemed to meet every one of our needs as a family. More so than any video game they could play at home, the memories we made together were one of a kind.

I can distinctly recall Mike swinging from the trees and cutting off small branches that were needed for the fire's kindling. When he realized we needed firewood, he lassoed his rope around the trunk of an old tree and tied it to the back of his truck's bumper. Once he drove away, the old rotten tree was quickly uprooted and pulled away from where it once stood. He drove through the woods and dragged this hundred-foot tree across the campgrounds. It seemed he played the part of Paul Bunyan perfectly. He raised an axe overhead, letting it drop quickly, and split the logs in two. He took pride placing the split wood into neat rows, which we used for our nightly campfires.

The sheer excitement he exuded as he lit the freshly cut firewood into flames was a bit overzealous. As he strategically stacked each log, giving them just the right angle to ignite, a blazing inferno took off. The orange flames went way up overhead and into the trees above us. It seemed the blazing heat was enough to ignite the surrounding forest on fire that night! Thankfully, we managed to get it somewhat under control just in time for dinner. Nevertheless, our steaks burnt to a crisp due to the fury of the hot wooden flames.

Early the next day, we walked up the hiking trails to see the expansive views from the peaks of the mountains. On that hike however, I couldn't make it up the steep rocks. I stayed behind and watched as Mike and the children led themselves up the mountain and out of sight. While they left me alone on what looked to be "Wildebeest Mountain", I was only equipped to take on Mother Nature with a small can of bug spray. As I sat alone in complete terror, I looked around and wondered if it was about lunchtime for some hungry animal.

As I anticipated, within only a few minutes of sitting still, a large swarm of mosquitos began their threatening buzz around my head. I dowsed them with my can of bug repellant, hoping they would relent from circling around me. The swarm of mosquitos seemed to have had super immunity to the bug spray. They merely laughed at my flimsy can of bug spray and continually gnawed away at my skin.

After I practically sprayed the entire can of bug spray at them, they finally left me alone. By about this time, an abrupt silence gave way to an entire array of horror scenes displayed throughout my mind. My decision to stay behind, instead of climbing up the steep rocks with my family, suddenly felt like a very bad idea. It seemed like it had been hours before they finally came hiking back down the mountain. I couldn't get down the mountain and back to the civilization of dirt and tents quick enough! Wow, there's a perspective moment of gratefulness.

Later that night, we washed up at the campgrounds and went out for a lovely dinner. I was somehow able to laugh about my killer mosquito experience, simply because I had just enough blood left to tell them about it. I may have looked a bit pale and anemic by this point, but I was just thankful to still be alive!

The crazy outdoor adventures in our lives all began well before we were married. The first glimpse of this strange desire to become one with nature all started with a trip to the Delaware River. This trip seemed innocent, until our attempts to raft down the river with a pool float didn't quite work out as we had planned. Of course, the adventures of pool floats don't usually include going over jagged rocks and rapids. Against my better judgement, Mike assured me that it was safe to take this tiny pool float down this giant river. Since I thought to myself that he was just the smartest man in the world, I trusted his judgment without any question.

We proceeded to glide down this massive river in nothing more than our flimsy pool raft. Swiftly, the current moved us amongst the forces of Mother Nature, while all along, I knew we were poorly equipped to even stay afloat. I noticed everyone else that passed by us on the river appeared to be in large sturdy rafts. Of course, they all watched us and wondered what in the world would happen next as we sped by them recklessly, and screaming out of fear for our lives, from our tiny float.

As we made our way further down the river, I noticed the choppy rapids quickly approaching us. I screamed out in sheer panic, as our flimsy raft bobbed up and down over them. I held onto our lunch cooler for dear life because I knew it was near lunch time, and I was somehow worried I'd have nothing left to eat! It's amazing how the optimism of my next meal never ceased to fail me, even amid my most embarrassing moments.

We bobbed up and down, until we nearly flew headfirst out of the raft ... lunch and all. I envisioned all our tuna sandwiches flying across the river and straight into a salmon's mouth. Ok, I admit that's a weird thought. As we bounced and bobbed over the swift rapids, we must have been a funny sight for that crowd, pointing at us down yonder. Miraculously, we somehow made it over the sharp edges of the rocks, laughing with the float still intact.

After the rapids began to dissipate, the reflection of the water mirrored the scenic images with its unsurpassable beauty. As we drifted down the river, its picture-perfect views and tranquility filled us with all that it had to offer. The simplicity of the majestic scenery seemed to wipe away all the uneasiness of the turbulent waters. As we made our way down the river, we continued to soak up the balminess of the sun's rays. It felt as if heaven and earth had just collided, until reality struck us. Suddenly becoming aware of the eerie silence, we sensed something just didn't seem right. In that moment it was silent, and my mind was playing that chilling sound of music, right before Jaws pops up out of the water, and shows its gruesomely sharp teeth. I can't explain how eerie it was to suddenly realize we were floating on a pool raft in a current that seemed to pull us somewhere out of reach.

We only heard the echo of our own voices out in the middle of nowhere and began wondering how we would ever get up to the roadside, and walk miles back to our car, where we originally put our raft in the water. We realized our raft had veered us far away from the road because the noise of the cars was no longer passing by. We had to be miles downriver and the only way back to our car was to try to find where it was parked somewhere back up on the road. The question that remained was how would we ever get back up to the road we could no longer see from downriver? We had no other choice, but to paddle upriver against the current, to get back to where we started. The same group of rafters that wondered what we were doing in a flimsy pool raft floated by us again, except this time we were trying to paddle up the river. I wondered what they must have been thinking about us by this point.

Where the waters were shallow, I forced Mike out of the raft and into the river to pull me upstream. Like a princess, I sat in the raft with my feet up, while I waved to the other rafters. I'd imagine we were quite a show for them by this point, as they watched him grumbling, pulling me up the river. After his ankles were beaten and bruised by the edges of the sharp rocks, we finally managed to reach a place where we heard the cars going by on the road again. But there was one major problem. Since we were a bit lower down on the river from where we originally began, we needed to climb up a much steeper cliff to get up to the road. I suddenly realized becoming an expert rock climber was a sheer necessity to get back up there. With no other choice in the matter, we proceeded up the steep cliff with our float and cooler in hand.

As we climbed upward, we grabbed onto the tree branches to help pull us up. I feared the flimsy branches would snap off, and all I could picture was rolling right down the hill, and back into the river. Finally, we climbed safely up to what I thought was the top of the cliff, only to find that there was a hundred-foot murky swamp that stood between us and what we thought was the road. The only way across the swamp was to walk across a slimy tree that had fallen from one side to the other. This looked just like a scene straight out of Indiana Jones! Mike thought it was safe to walk across this moldy, slippery, crumbling old log. I absolutely refused to walk across it. After all, I had just finished sweating it out with the art of rock climbing. I didn't have another newfound desire to walk across this narrow log like a tight rope in a circus act. The only other option we had was to climb up a much steeper cliff further up the river, which would allow us to finally get up to the road.

Being we already succeeded at our first rock climbing experience, we opted to go further up the river and climb some more. We walked back down the hill and into the river again. There, more ankle gashing and grumbling continued, as I remained all comfy in the float. Eventually we made it to the steep incline and climbed up the treacherous terrain of what seemed to be a mini-Mount Everest. Once again, I found myself slipping and sliding on the loose gravel beneath my feet. I grabbed onto the tree branches to avoid doing tumble saults back down the cliff. With one step at a time, we made it to the clearing of the roadside. We walked up the road a way, and finally around the bend, we spotted our car. I quickly got in it, and we drove home in nothing but sheer silence, bewildered by the day of unexpected events. I knew if I even just looked at him, it would not have been with an endearing expression on my face. I vowed to myself I would never return to the river again in that darn pool float unless I was being filmed for new reality T.V. show.

Although this river roadside trip turned into a giant fiasco, it was not the one and only. On many other occasions we found ourselves in a bit of a dilemma as well. The one that stood out in my mind that went completely awry was a camping trip alongside a picturesque lake.

It all began with the optimism of a bright sunny day. So, we decided to take a rowboat out onto the lake. With our life vests intact, we stepped down into the boat and left the shore behind. As we rowed along the inlets, we saw the land from a new perspective ... FAR AWAY.

Many birds soared overhead, as we watched for the chance of an eagle sighting. While paddling along, Mike decided to row us into the middle of this enormous lake. Just as we rowed into the center, the sky began covering us with the threat of dark rain clouds. Out of nowhere, the winds began blowing and the waves grew larger. I quickly hung onto my children, fearing that we would all fly overboard.

As we bobbed up and down, the sky lit with a fury of lightning bolts that zigzagged around us. The rolls of thunder, followed by a display of vicious strikes, grew louder. The waves began slapping against the side of the boat. The thunder quickly followed with a booming sound that seemed to echo for miles. The wind's resistance held us from rowing back to shore. I held onto the kids tightly and yelled "Get down and batten down the hatches" (well there weren't any hatches). Instead, we huddled down at the bottom of the shallow rowboat, with the rain slapping us in the face, and Mike trying desperately to row us back to shore. He was rowing against the current vigorously, and yet, we were going nowhere fast.

With a startling yell, I cried out to him, "Look what you've done now! I didn't want to row into the middle of this giant lake in the first place!" I thought to myself, "This is it, this is the end of our lives, and we are either going to get struck by lightning or drown." I really didn't enjoy the thought of any of these options. So, there we were out on a wide-open lake, unprotected in a dinky metal rowboat. I began wondering what it was with us and dinky boats anyway. If I ever got in a boat again it was going to be in a giant yacht! I never really liked boats in the first place, and although I was hesitant to get in it, I tried to be brave, and this is what I got for it. I reassured myself that it was a beautiful sunny day, and the waters were calm. It seemed like the ideal conditions to take an innocent trip along the lakeside. Yet, there I was huddled up at the bottom of this boat yelling to myself, "I told you this wasn't a good idea!!" Honestly, my thoughts alone back then would have been enough to cause us all to sink!

I don't know whether it was the look of shear panic on my face, or the look in my eyes that I was angry with my husband, but he began rowing the boat as hard as he could. By this point, he was sweating it out, as the kids and I were shivering, being dowsed by the cold waves pouring into the boat. The sky finally opened with its torrential rain and drenched every inch of us. While the freezing wind smashed the cold beads of rain against our skin, it felt as if we would never make it back to shore again. I was praying so hard and saying, "God, couldn't this just be a drizzle?" I was beginning to feel a bit like the skipper from Gilligan's Island, as the swaying from the large waves were about to capsize the boat.

As I lifted my head, I noticed Mike trying to stand up. He was attempting to row the boat even harder. Suddenly, I heard a loud snap and watched one of the oars he was paddling with crack in half. I thought to myself, "This simply CANNOT be happening!" He quickly tried to catch the paddle. No such luck. We watched the furious current of the lake drag it into the giant swallows of the undertow. The look on his face was like, "UH OH, she's going to throw me overboard NOW!" Honestly, I took a moment and considered it, only I knew I'd have to row myself back to shore with only one paddle in hand, and that idea was simply out of the question.

The next thing I realized, as he began rowing with one paddle, was that the boat was spinning around in circles! As if I hadn't had enough excitement for the day, I suddenly found myself bobbing up and down and spinning around in circles like a ride at the fun park. Except for one thing, I wasn't having fun at all. All I could do was yell out "OH MY GOD, MAKE IT STOP SPINNING!" I held onto my kids tightly, and as he rowed from side to side, he finally gained control over the boat.

As I looked up, I saw people far off on the distant shore watching us with the look of concern on their faces. There we were once again, as the central theme of attraction, looking like a bunch of buffoons. I remember thinking that I only wished we had a flare gun to set off for a rescue squad. Right about that time, I noticed there wasn't anyone else out on the lake. I raised an eyebrow and thought to myself, "Did they know something we didn't?" I believe Mike had the same exact thought and gave it his best shot to get us back to shore.

He continued rowing furiously, and finally we managed to make it back to the docks safely. We felt a bit weathered and weary, as we stepped out of the boat, and onto dry land. And wouldn't you know it, no sooner did we get safely on land, that the sun peaked out from behind the gray clouds as if to say, "JUST KIDDING!" I don't know why, but for a moment, I wondered if a camera crew was filming us foolishly floundering around out there in the eye of the storm. I thought the worst-case scenario would be if we made it onto a T.V. episode of the world's silliest people captured on video.

Over the countless number of camping adventures, I tolerated an entire array of unexpected wildlife. Every day was led by the freakiness of Mother Nature. Many nights, while I sat relaxing by the campfire there were giant bugs whizzing past my head. They sounded just like a fighter plane coming in for an attack on my ear drums. It was inevitable that I would foolishly make a spectacle of myself with one of my own idiotic dance routines to swat these giant bugs away from my head. I'd spend the rest of the night removing gooey bug juice from my hair and maybe even in between my teeth (I'm not sure).

Of course, I could always count on the shadows of strange beasts creeping around our tent later at night. It felt more like a remake of a Jurassic Park movie, rather than having a peaceful night with crickets chirping me off to sleep. I really wouldn't have been the least bit surprised if King Kong himself swung out of a tree to pick the bugs out of my hair. My imagination went completely wild!

It was never a good hair day with bug juice melded into my hair. The sweltering heat, dampness, and pouring rain only made matters worse. I had only a small tent as my shelter on a muddy campground. Let me just add that I was a high maintenance woman, so camping was especially challenging for me. However, I made no excuses when it came time to bear the elements for my family's sake. I survived by bringing along my twenty pound make up trunk wherever I went. Everyone thought my makeup trunk was just a large tackle box for fishing anyway.

Coincidently, there weren't any luxuries for me to get lost in for very long either. Many times, I found myself showering alongside large and hairy bugs that I couldn't even begin to describe. Allowing my body to touch anything except the single drop of water coming from the rusty old shower head was certainly enough to make me scream out in sheer terror. The number of germs that accumulated on those campground shower curtains were as nasty as nasty gets. There came a point that I opted for the sandy lake water as my bath instead. As for the toilet accommodations, well let's just say that many times, we made our own facilities outside, along with all the other camping enthusiasts trying to make friends with Mother Nature.

Did I have to become the outdoorsy type for the sake my family's adventurous excursions? Well yes, I did. Quite frankly, I'm surprised that I survived it all in one piece. Still, it was worth every single inconvenience and nasty disaster. I know I could've taken an ordinary vacation at a luxury resort hotel, and sipped on a sweet tea, but the unexpected ventures with Mother Nature, still hold a place in our hearts today. Even during my darkest days, the memories of us all being together, created a light that could never fade away.

Chapter 11

Getting to Know Her

Shannon's need for independence in her first year of life was already apparent. On her first birthday, I bought her a baby doll and toy stroller. She had barely begun walking on her own. She steadied herself by leaning on the stroller, and it allowed her to walk independently. She pushed the stroller back and forth along the entire length of the house.

She was so determined, but as she forcefully pushed her stroller to get where she wanted, it managed to wedge itself underneath a piece of furniture. I tried to move it for her, but she pulled my hand away quickly as if to say, "I will do it myself!" She maneuvered the stroller with such determination that it displayed her willful personality. Her conviction was, "I'm going somewhere and I'm doing it by myself!" I had a feeling in that moment this kid was certainly going places one day without the help of anyone.

She was only twenty-one months old when my son was born. She had a natural way of nurturing him, as if she were already a mother. When I first placed him in her arms, her mouth opened wide, and from ear to ear she grinned with a giant smile. They were inseparable from the time he arrived, until the day that she left. She never told him anything about her plans to run away. He was just as devastated by her betrayal as we all were.

When she was two years old, I decided to send her to preschool. She was eager to learn new things every day. She awaited her first day of school with sheer excitement. I placed her on the school bus, and she didn't even look back for me. I can remember thinking how independent she seemed. I felt sad that day because she never turned around to say goodbye, and yet, I was happy that she was eager to go without any hesitation. I knew there was something different about her from the moment she rode away and never looked back. Remembering this departing moment, it seemed ironic that years later she would get on a train leaving her hometown without ever looking back again. As I later thought of these moments, I realized how they mimicked one another. It was that day on the bus that would eventually reveal something so much deeper than I ever thought.

The years flew by and the next thing I knew she was in grade school. She was a unique little girl. She had a group of friends that she never really seemed to fit in with. They were the typical girly-girl type. She was the tom-boy type that liked to play sports with all the boys. She was not the least bit concerned about how her hair looked or what kind of clothes she wore. Even when the other girls made remarks towards her differences, she did not conform to their ways.

She never seemed interested in taking the path of least resistance. She seemed to thrive on being different than everyone else. Peer pressure wasn't any issue for her. She refused to succumb to it. She made the decision to be her own person from a very young age. She was always beyond her years with a mature confidence, unlike the rest of her friends.

In both her middle school and high school years, she was a bright and conscientious student. I never had to oversee one assignment given to her. Over the years, she worked very hard in all her classes and her grades were above average. She was self-motivated to complete any task given to her. She spent most of her time in her room doing homework, or so I thought. If she wasn't doing her homework, she was at school playing sports. I had only the best of reports about her from all her teachers.

There wasn't a day that she had ever given me any trouble. She abided by her curfews (which were far earlier than all her friends) and respected our parental authority. The friends that she hung around with were mostly the girls that played sports. Occasionally, they went out socially during the weekends. She always told me where she was going, and I knew when I could expect her home.

She was helpful around the house with chores and seemed to like spending time with me, until everything in my life went haywire. She kept her room spotless and orderly without my asking her to do so. In all the years of raising her, she never once asked me for anything unnecessary. She never really had the need for things; she just stuck with the bare necessities.

At seventeen, she began working as a bus girl in a restaurant. Within a short period of time, she had worked her way up to become a waitress. We bought her a brand-new car as a measure of how grateful we were that she was such a responsible daughter. She never abused the privilege of having this new car we bought for her.

She began saving every single penny that she made from the day she started working. She worked for over twelve hours each day on the weekends. She worked every single hour they offered her, including most weekends when her friends were out having fun. I hadn't any clue that her dedication to this job was because she was saving her money for the runaway plan.

In her senior year, I did notice that she seemed distant towards me. She went to school, played sports, worked, and spent the rest of the time in her room on her computer. Our time together seemed to become more limited as the year progressed. Our conversations were increasingly more vacant and distant. I wondered if the pressure of the upcoming year was building with the anticipation and uncertainty in her life.

On a few occasions, I tried speaking with her about future. I knew something didn't seem quite right, but I hit a brick wall every time I brought the subject up. I wanted her to know I was aware she wasn't being open with me about her life. I just couldn't seem to break through the walls she built around herself because of our difference of opinions in the past.

I idealized my own vision of how I thought she should be as a little girl. I was the girly-girl type when I was growing up, and it was the only way I knew how to be. Dressing up in my mother's old high heel shoes, and playing with makeup and baby dolls, was how I spent all the days of my youth. When she turned out to be completely the opposite of me, I hadn't a clue what to do with her.

By the time she was in her teen years, I really didn't have an understanding about her wants and desires in life. I was completely narrow-minded within my own beliefs as to what I thought a young girl should be like. I guess what I am really saying is that I was trying to make her into something she wasn't.

Looking back, I can see how our difference of opinions began creating division between us. Eventually she began shutting down on me because I never supported her own desires. Instead, I pushed my own ideas on her. I had inadvertently supported the girly-girls in school that were mean to her because of her individuality. I know she spent years questioning herself as to why she was so different than the rest of the girly-girls.

Looking back, I tried to place myself in her shoes and everything she must have been going through while feeling unsupported. Eventually she shut the windows to her heart and kept secrets from me. Initially, her runaway seemed heartless to me, but over time, I felt the anguish she must have faced without having my support. She had so many desires wrapped up inside of her that she couldn't even begin

79

to share with me. Over the years, this became a giant wall that distanced us emotionally, and eventually placed us on opposite sides of the map.

Chapter 12

Missing Pieces

As the years of my life progressed, facing every day became a giant chore. I lived with a constant lack of fulfillment inside of me. I was becoming more exhausted than I had the energy to endure. It weighed me down at a rate that was unbearable to uphold. It was as if I was carrying the weight of my unsatisfied life, and the things that had gone wrong, with every step that I took. No matter what I tried to do to change, it only seemed to make matters worse. It didn't seem to matter where I was, or what I was doing, there was always this unsatisfied anxious feeling inside of me.

The years of raising my children were undoubtedly the greatest part of my life. Yet somehow there was still something lost within me. I never had a feeling of being complete or worthy of more as an individual. I always had this feeling that I was going around in circles from one thing to another, without ever finding the missing pieces inside of me.

I began realizing that if I had developed a personal relationship with God, the anguish I endured wouldn't have ever existed. In virtually every aspect of my life, I settled for much less than what God wanted for me. This left me always wanting more in my life, never knowing exactly what it was.

Consequently, I spent years pursuing more of the wrong things which were all to no avail.

Shannon's life was parallel to mine in that she had missing pieces inside of her as well. She desperately tried searching for these pieces by running far away. Both of us searched aimlessly for something to fulfill us but didn't know where to begin to find it. During our own pain, we hurt the people that we loved the most. We were lost and hadn't any idea how to solve the problems within our own lives.

She ran away believing this was her only way to start a new life. She convinced herself she wasn't running away; but rather was running towards her dreams. She had not yet realized that no matter how far we run, we have already packed all our troubles inside of us. There was no escape from the turmoil within our hearts unless we dealt with the root cause of our own painful issues.

As she began growing up, she became greatly aware that I was longing for more in my life. Over the years, she witnessed my unsuccessful attempts at trying to fill the emptiness inside of me. I became an expert at pursuing all the wrong things for my life. As a result, I emotionally shut down as a way of coping with this endless feeling of failure.

With the uncertainty of my life's direction, I became distant in all my relationships. I was in my own world, trapped amongst the many negative beliefs that I held onto about myself. My negative thoughts about myself defeated any efforts of finding my true self. Like a poison spreading, my viewpoints about everyone else became negative as well. My own negativity began leading me down many wrong roads and veered me straight into a ditch of depression.

With God at my side, I found the courage through my faith to first identify, and finally face these negative thoughts and feelings of myself. God continued revealing all the problems that arose from my negative state of mind. Suddenly, it seemed to hit me square in the face. I knew that I had to stop running from my own state of inner turmoil, so that my daughter would stop running from me.

The constant tension between my inner state and outer state tugged on me in multiple directions every day in a state of mass confusion. My actions and behaviors were far from what God had planned for me and it was time for me to undo the lost woman I had become. I concluded the woman that I had been portraying on the outside, looked nothing like the one on the inside, and it was tearing me apart. It was time to start taking my faith more seriously, to place my identity in the promises of God and change from the inside out. I worked hard, and relentlessly, to begin changing my life. There seemed to be a sense of urgency, knowing that Shannon was lost too, and needed to finally have a stable mother that she could trust to rely on.

Chapter 13

Have Mercy on Me

As I explored the depths of my soul with the help of my mentor Sammy, the pressure of all my realities spun me into a whirlwind of painful emotions. This process provoked anger inside of me that I was unaware of having. I saw myself behave in such a way that brought out the absolute worst in me. It revealed a dark side of me, hidden underneath the years of hurt and disappointment in my life.

During this time, the angry, bitter, and broken woman I really was inside reared its ugly head. I began to dislike the mentorship, but he continued to provoke my anger throughout this process. Regardless of what I felt, I continued working with him anyway. Initially, this process seemed to only exacerbate my issues and I wanted to quit! But it was obvious to me that he knew what he was doing because I was finally facing some of the truth about myself. He continued dealing with the issues inside of me, until eventually it smoothed out the sharp edges of my disposition. Well, most of them anyway.

The process was painfully real, causing all the things from the past that were hidden away inside of me to finally come out. When I prayed for a spiritual coach, I envisioned us floating around on white fluffy clouds, while gazing at sunsets together. I watched this bubble of dreams quickly dissipate, realizing it wasn't at all what I had imagined it would be. Instead, I ended up with spiritual coaching that felt more like a spiritual truth sentence. I would either die from it, or I would survive, and it would change my life.

I whined and prayed relentlessly to God for a new coach daily. As I continued to pray and soak myself in self-pity, my heart poured out the same thing over and over again- not to give up this fight. I sensed God was saying to me "the only other choice you have is to veer from the designated path that I have already laid out for you." I mean after all; spiritual coaches don't usually just drop into your life from three thousand miles away. I suddenly felt silly for trying to rearrange God's plans, knowing that this was already an answered prayer.

I had this deep knowing that I still had additional issues to resolve in my life, so I made the decision to stay on God's chosen course. By this time, I was aggravated with this counseling all the time. I just wanted everything to go my way or no way. Nevertheless, Sammy didn't play that game with me. I thought that I was going to tell him what to do and exactly how to do it. Well, that didn't work out according to my plans either. As a matter of fact, I learned that being mentored wasn't about having control over the kind of help that I required. On most days, I felt like I was turned upside down and inside out. I tried to fool myself with the sense of having control over his God-given authority, and it only made matters worse. God placed this person in my life, and I knew that I had to submit to the process to begin to find the way out of all my troubles and sorrows.

I was still such a whiner anyway and continued grumbling to God, pleading for Him to find someone else to mentor me (as if I knew what was best). I tried to quit seeking his council, only to find out later that I needed Sammy back for his help. It was outright embarrassing, groveling back to him, and begging for his mercy repeatedly. I couldn't help but notice that my behavior was quite double-minded and unstable, and it became more obvious this was the struggle throughout my life. Eventually, I had finally come to terms with allowing God's plan to work in my life through this intense process of discovering the truth, and I knew by this point that my own plans were simply not the answer for solving any of my problems.

Over the next several months, I was still a bit aggravated with having to finally see myself truthfully. Yet, I desperately wanted to rise above the madness within me to be the winner at the end of this journey.

During facing all the evil things that had held me back from living my life, I had a God-given idea that felt as if it came down and hit me in the head like a lightning bolt ... it was something profound that just clicked in my mind and would change my life forever. I knew that I had so much to share with the world about my own journey with God! I had a vision from God in that very moment that my life was a story about confronting my sins and repenting of them. This vision was as plain as day and writing a book about being a conqueror of my own inner battles became a passionate desire to help others. So far, I survived confronting many of my inner battles and knew something good had to come of it all. I felt like a true warrior, and I needed to write about every life changing event since the day Shannon had run away from home.

I cringed at the thought of even admitting that having the madness provoked from inside of me was a good thing. Somehow, the pressure that was put on me during this time led to my faith in God, and eventually He managed to bring out the best in me.

I must encourage those reading this not to give up just because of the uncomfortableness associated with facing the problems we have been running from for most of our lives. My plan was to keep on living my life without ever really facing my problems, but far off in the background of my mind there was always something screaming," let me out". My emotional pain was always bearing down on me, reminding me of what a failure I thought I had become. I would try to drown it all out by numbing myself with many glasses of wine. I convinced myself that facing the truth about who I turned out to be was way too overwhelming to ever face alone ... and I was right about that because we cannot face the cold hard truth, and the shame of all the things we have done, without turning to God first.

In some strange way, my dissatisfaction with life had become somewhat of a comfort zone. Changing would have meant facing the enormous mountain of the horrifying things that I did ... but I simply did not have enough strength to face the ugliness of it all alone, and I believe that none of us do. I believe it is only when we are willing to accept the gracious gift from God to finally have that moment of holiness with Him alone, and discover who we truly are, that we can change.

Up until this time, God knew I had done such a great job of avoiding all the skeletons in my closet. Nevertheless, He managed to find just the right person to help me begin to change. Even though there were days I found myself on my knees praying that God would have mercy on me, and I wouldn't need to hear from Sammy again, I knew sooner or later I would. I always had this sense of being under what I referred to as "spiritual surveillance." It seemed that as God watched over me, a phone call would manage to come through from Sammy during my worst possible moments. I finally had to be honest with myself though, knowing I couldn't move forward in my life without completing this process first.

For several months, I was pressured to face everything in my past that was left undone. Over the years, the heaviness of my personal baggage weighed me down, and closed in on me. I was exhausted trying to defend all that I had denied that was pent up inside of me. Up until everything was completely shattered, I tried desperately to deny anything was wrong, but I knew I couldn't go on like this any longer. It was time to face the demons inside that were haunting me from as far back as I could recall. The bottom line was that I was desperate for the truth!

Over the years, my emotional state became almost paralyzing. It stood around me like giant walls of concrete. I built a protective barrier from the ugliest reminders of my past. It was all there in the background of my mind, but I kept right on running, trying to hide from the agony of it all. When I finally began to face the pain reflecting at me, I realized it was slowly eating away at my soul over the course of my life. My secrets finally came pouring out of me during this crucial time of my life, and I began realizing it was in the power of confessing my sins that was the only way to heal. There were many things I was hiding from everyone, and was too ashamed to admit, even to myself. I was never brave enough to confront the truth about what I had done to destroy my life, and everyone else's.

Looking back, I realized there were a billion negative thoughts and beliefs that I had about myself that led me to do horrendous things that I never imagined I would do. The belief system that I accumulated were through many generational curses passed down to me. Unfortunately, they began defining my life at a very young age and in a very negative way. I stepped into most things that I did, already believing that I was sure to fail, and on some deeper level, my mind said to me, "just go ahead and fulfill that prophecy." I couldn't even consider doing the many things in my life that I should have done. I felt cornered and trapped underneath these generational strongholds in my life that caused me to suffer with anxiety and depression. My anxieties over the years were on a rampage as they slowly, but surely, caused my life to crash into pieces.

Meditating on the Word of God allowed me to have the faith that was necessary to overcome these challenging obstacles. Over the months, I noticed that the depression and anxiety were progressively beginning to diminish. This was a growing process, and as I took it one step at a time, I knew that there were many other mountains to climb.

Looking back over my childhood, I attended church every Sunday and quite frankly, I never learned anything practical. A few prayers and some religious rules and regulations were about all that I walked away with. I felt no connection to the Catholic Church, and I decided to abandon my faith at the age of seventeen. I had no other resources that I knew of to help pull me out from underneath my dreadful teenage years of insecurity. Unfortunately, I continued to live with my own mixed-up beliefs about myself throughout most of my adulthood.

I collected years of people's opinions and used them to identify myself. I hadn't any other knowledge or understanding of who I really was inside. My school years were the most detrimental of all. I was labeled with a multitude of learning disabilities, including ADHD because I was unable to focus with all that was going on in my home environment. I was perfectly capable of learning anything, but not with the chaotic environment of my family, filled with anxiety, as I was growing up.

As I embarked on this new journey, the Holy Spirit became a teacher that surpassed any type of teaching that I had ever experienced. The Holy Spirit spoke to my heart and understood me like no one ever did before. As this small voice inside of me spoke, it led me on this unforgettable journey of adventure, helping me to discover who I truly was as a wholehearted woman. My experience became just as it was written in 1 John 2:27, "But you have received the Holy Spirit, and he lives within you, so you don't need anyone to teach you what is true. For the spirit teaches you everything you need to know, and what he teaches is true. Just as he has taught you, remain in fellowship with Christ."

Without the Holy Spirit residing in me, my adult life had become nothing more than an imprisonment of feeling worthless. I was filled with nothing more than the misfortunes of my childhood, but with God's love upon me, I was finally able to have an inner healing from the wounds of my past. I refused to go on living my life allowing people to define who I was anymore, or what I was capable of accomplishing.

I was most certain that it would not have been possible for me to have written this book if I continued listening to people's opinions about anything. This book was written on the sole basis of the Holy Spirit guiding me into a life of freedom. The pure miracle of writing this book was that at first, I lacked the education to be able to put it into a legible format, until I believed that anything was possible with God. Along this faith filled journey, God's story for my life gracefully unfolded the truth. I spent hour upon hour relentlessly writing down every word, as I was inspired by the amazing changes within me. I believe that my book will exemplify how a vision from God can give us the faith to believe in our hopes and dreams for ourselves and our families.

The healing that I received from God in all the damaged areas of my life were managing to remove the barriers that held me back from truly living. My restoration opened a river of desires inside of me, freeing my soul and allowing me to become passionate about my life. I was completely unaware that the previous decades caused me to remain dormant, not knowing my identity in Christ.

In addition, I realized how my insecurities affected my marriage and I spent years depending on Mike to do for me what I felt I was incapable of doing myself. I lived behind him to cover up the failures in my life, but the hurt from my past was beginning to fade, and the major roadblocks in my life that kept me held captive to the feeling of failure and worthlessness, were becoming a more of a distant memory. The cold feeling of being frozen in time, as I faced my fears and insecurities, was only for a short season of my life. I was finding glimpses of hope each day, as my future looked more promising than ever before.

Chapter 14

Paths of Life

Six months had passed since the dreary day that Shannon had run away from home in search of her dreams. Over the months, I had spoken with her about my own mentorship, and how it began to transform my life. On a few occasions, I mentioned to her that mentoring could help her too. To my surprise she accepted the proposition to get help from him. She probably had just enough time of being out on her own, and life's opportunities probably weren't knocking at her door, so by this stage of the game, she was open to a new direction. The way that God had lined things up for us, in His perfect timing, truly created miracles!

During the previous months of her runaway, she was downright adamant about not accepting anyone's help. She was completely emphatic about having her independence. I believe by this point in time however, she realized this was a golden opportunity, which she could not deny herself. This was a gift from God, which could lead her life in the direction she desired.

As I thought about the direction of my own life, there was simply no denying that her runaway was one of my darkest days. Everything came to a crashing halt on that same day. It seemed all my years of unhappiness caught up with me in that one moment that I realized she was gone. It was at this time that God began uncovering the whole slew of problems in my life. The experience was surreal. As God touched upon the painful areas, I became dreadfully aware that I had inadvertently placed an excessive amount of emotional reliance on others. I was trying to derive everything that was missing inside of me from my relationships. I expected others to do for me what I denied doing for myself, and I relied solely upon them to fill in the missing pieces of my life.

The multitude of problems that I suffered from stemmed from my own lack of identity. I spent years projecting my unhappiness onto others, rather than taking responsibility for myself. What a complete drain on my husband this really was, and to somehow feel as if he had to fulfill a role he never could, was really sabotage on my part.

I hid behind all my relationships in my family, vicariously trying to live out my own identity through each of them. On a deep level, I somehow believed there were unique individual parts in each of my family members that provided them with everything I wished I could become within my own life. I believed that I didn't have what it took to feel worthy of doing anything special. I was simply nothing at all without them. I was stuck in the middle of always trying to attach myself to something, or someone else, in search of my true self. I was completely unaware that what I truly needed was my own God-given identity.

My relationships were falling apart at the seams. No matter what effort others went to trying to help me, it didn't seem to fill the emptiness inside my soul. The relentless expectations that I placed on the people closest to me slowly caused the relationships to crack. I believe my unreasonable expectations played a large part in the pressure my daughter felt from me, and the role that she no longer wanted to fill. This behavior was also one of the major causes of destruction in my relationship with Mike.

Although being a wife and a mother were my roles, I was led to believe they were the sole reason for my existence. These were both very important roles, and I don't want to sound as if I am undermining their value in my life, but I never took the time to find out who I truly was beforehand, and the devastating result was that I felt broken and incomplete during the years of being a wife and a mother. Although I knew deep down inside that I was called to be something more, I had no idea what I was searching for.

After Shannon ran away, I felt as if I was unsuccessful at fulfilling one of the only things, I believed I could accomplish during my lifetime. Mothering meant everything to me since the day she was born, and suddenly my life was pulled out from beneath me. I was at a complete loss. Every day, since this journey began, I needed to press forward in my battle against the lies and negative thoughts of feeling like a complete failure. Although my life had begun to improve, it was because every minute of the day, I fought the fear driven thoughts of where my life might be taking me with the ill feelings of no hope insight.

Her runaway uncovered my belief that I felt like I was a complete failure as a wife and mother. I felt utterly hopeless in every area that I faced. Even so, I continued to press forward with my faith knowing this was the only way that I could conquer my own negative beliefs from the past. It took time and unrelenting effort to conquer my thoughts and anxieties. I knew the victory awaiting me relied solely upon many giant leaps of faith. Step by step, I began cultivating new perspectives with all of God's promises.

I started by clearing the slate of every wrongdoing in my life and tried to begin all over again. I cut myself off from the activities of the world and forged ahead with a quiet trust in the solitude of my daily worship. This was a true test of faith, and I believed that I would finally receive everything my heart truly desired one day. My stillness before the Lord became my daily worship that I looked forward to every day. I yearned for a new place in my life, and desperately needed God's direction. Slowly but surely, my solitude began revealing glimpses of new pathways for my future.

Over the months, I began sensing that what I lacked on the inside was beginning to change. As God began filling the emptiness inside my soul through the power of His promises, my sense of utter hopelessness began healing. The power of the Word was creating a new life inside of me. It was a path that led the way to relational harmony with God, as my true purpose in life. This new foundation of stability began emanating from the inside out. I knew that I was no longer on the path of destruction, but rather the path of life.

Chapter 15

The Process of Elimination

My spiritual journey led me to every area of my life in need of restoration. Up to this point, I relied upon my own resources to resolve my problems. This led to a lifetime of failures that were left under a giant pile of unresolved issues, but I took it one step at a time, unveiling every single one of them. God had given me a snapshot of my life and everything that had gone wrong. I was becoming more aware of all my unresolved issues, and I was finally ready to face every one of them.

I was no longer relying upon my own resources, as the Holy Spirit revealed to me the many areas in my life that needed healing. In the back of my mind, I had a checklist from beginning to end. This cleared away any kind of uncertain thoughts such as "where do I even BEGIN to be able change my life?" The course of direction was made very clear deep within me. It was almost as if every move was already planned out for me. I may not have had all the details, but I knew that God would show me every step of the way.

My first task on God's checklist was what I referred to as the "weeding out process." I began by eliminating the meaningless things in all areas of my life. I knew these areas of my life only perpetuated the feeling of emptiness inside

98

of me. They just didn't have a place in my life anymore. I began with the process of elimination by relinquishing quite a few major things that God revealed were a hindrance to my life.

The first area that called upon my heart was the decision to relinquish all my bad habits that were leading to a sinful lifestyle. I also knew that I needed to disassociate from any bad influence, which were most of the people in my personal life. Another area of my life that God was calling to my attention was the need to give up my excessive shopping excursions (ouch that one really hurt).

At one point, I was buying more makeup than one face could ever wear in a lifetime. My makeup box weighed in at an all-time high of almost twenty pounds. This was more than my dog weighed for crying out loud! Who could possibly have needed all that makeup? I did, however, really enjoy playing with makeup, so I prayed that God would just let me keep some of it.

The weeding out of excessive things eventually became a long list of things to do. This included giving up my expensive dream car, the immediate want for a bigger home, the excessive use of credit cards, watching and listening to inappropriate television and music, days of needless texting, compulsive internet shopping, shoe shopping, endless scrolling through Facebook, Instagram, and Twitter, to ending my day by numbing the unfulfillment inside myself with alcohol. I know this would sound to most people like quite a sudden way of finally finding myself. However, I

99

knew this was exactly what I needed to do to get to the root of my problems. It is not that wanting a dream home, texting, or shopping is a bad thing, unless it is used as a way of escaping from dealing with our problems.

For me, these were all just used as distractions in my life that were leading me far from God's purpose. Apparently, God wanted my undivided attention, and it was obvious that He no longer wanted me to live in a numb state of denial.

Even though I thought this new way of life would bore me, I realized the bad habits that I was about to face were only temporary fixes, and they only made me feel more worthless over time. You may be familiar with the term "quick fix." Well, there wasn't anything quick about the fixes in my life that I needed to make, until I obeyed what God was leading me to do. The changes I needed required my willingness to endure whatever sacrifices it took to change my ways.

The process of eliminating all the fruitless things in my life was not comfortable or easy. After all, it was mostly the meaningless things in my life that filled my days. Even though I didn't understand why God asked me to remove most everything from my life, I didn't complain about it. I asked God to show me the new path for my life, and I vowed to trust God and commit to the road He was leading me on.

When God told me to remove these worthless things from my life, I abided in His request and removed them. My faith was accelerating all in God's perfect timing, and I was able to press forward to the greater parts of my journey. Initially, the days left me feeling vacant, but I continued to remove most everything standing in my way. I knew that I couldn't grow with my old comfy habits. Yet, somehow, I found myself feeling even more lost than ever before, as my habitual behaviors no longer filled my days. Nevertheless, I was left with hope and belief in God's promises for a greater future. My only job was simply to believe that I was being led to far greater places than ever before.

As I finished this stage of the elimination process, God asked me to reflect upon my life. He wanted me to face who I believed I was without all the distractions. The way that I was living was an attempt of fulfilling what I thought were my dreams as a young girl. They once were a part of the ultimate dream for my life. Money had become a form of worship, and I realized that I spent years chasing after material things. Even though it may have appeared that I had it all on the outside, I was beginning to discover that I wasn't feeling the slightest bit fulfilled inside. The temporary fixes that money provided were leading my life down a dark and dreary hole. The life I was living was a façade, a make-believe land of the lost. It was only a sad attempt to cover up the pain of emptiness living inside of me.

This new revelation brought me to the scripture 1 John 2:15-17, "Do not love or cherish the world or the things in the world. Anyone who has love for the world does not have love for the Father. For all that is in the world- the lust of the flesh (craving for sensual gratification), and the lust of the eyes (greedy longings of the mind), and the pride of life (assurance of one's own resources or in the stability of earthly things), these do not come from the Father but are from the world. And the world passes away and disappears, and with it the forbidden cravings (the passionate desires, the lust) of it, but he who does the Will of God and carries out his purpose in his life abides and remains forever."

Over time, I became greatly aware that I was living to satisfy the flesh. I was suffering the consequences of gratifying my passionate desires, lusting, and longing after things that were completely selfish. My wayward life only left me with nothing more than the harsh reality of these shallow hungers left inside of me. There was no denying the unquenchable thirst for a deeper meaning in my life. Unlike living in the flesh, the leading of the Holy Spirit felt unlimited with endless possibilities for my future. As I began trusting in God's will, I was no longer scared of facing the truth about my life and changing my ways. Just as Jesus knew who He was and where He was going, I was beginning to know the same.

Chapter 16

Beauty and the Beast

The realization of never knowing who I was continued to dig deeper into my wounds. I had come to a point in my life where I was unrecognizable, even to myself. By this point, I only identified with the feeling of being a horrible wife and mother. Although I was once proud to be both, no one else, including myself, seemed to be impressed lately. Over the years, society did nothing but downplay my role as a stay-at-home wife and mother to the point of shame, and I began to question my desire to fulfill these roles.

The only other thing that I was left with was the power to use my external appearance to gain attention from others. Even from the time I was a little girl, this type of recognition was the only kind I ever had. The pressure of looking somewhat like a Barbie doll was my only other image to hold onto. Even though I knew I had more to offer than just being attractive to others, no one else ever seemed to notice this part of me. I felt like a mere shell of some insignificant object that had no depth or meaning. I would literally fuss over my looks for hours so that I could show off this outer beauty that everyone else seemed to admire. At any social occasion, I hung onto Mike feeling so insecure, wondering if any other woman's beauty would stand out over mine.

I was the apple of my father's eye while I was growing up. Even in his eyes, the recognition of my beauty seemed to be the winning prize, but on any given day that I decided not to wear any makeup, my parents would inform me that I looked as pale as a ghost (in other words, I needed makeup). My hair was another topic of discussion for everyone. Those were the days of the Farrah Faucet hair style, and it was "the image" to uphold. It took me at least forty-five minutes of blow drying my hair to have "The Look." Well, I had the look alright, but this look had failed to fulfill the deepest parts of me.

Throughout the years, even though my beauty seemed to be something everyone else was in awe of seeing, I was not. When I looked in the mirror, all I saw was an ugly side of me that no one else knew about. I had no idea what everyone else was seeing in me, when all I saw were the major flaws. They could not see the inside of me, but I felt the ugliness living inside of me every day. The way I felt about myself just didn't seem to add up to what they were admiring about me on the outside. I thought they were all just nuts. Even on my best days, I could find any number of reasons to justify that there wasn't anything beautiful about me. It was all the "cover girl" look and what I began calling, "fake up."

The pressure to uphold the appearance of my external beauty was suffocating. As the years went on, so did more of the fake up (makeup). I honestly believed that I was so ugly that I tried to hide it underneath layers and layers of concealer and foundation. The uglier I felt on the inside, the more

104

makeup I used to cover it up on the outside. I started to use so much makeup that it looked like I had a layer of spackle on my face, but it was all about to crack and reveal what was underneath.

I was a BIG fan of the shopping network channels on TV and ordered just about every beauty gadget that you could imagine. I had a facial hair remover that sounded a bit like a chain saw when I turned it on. Wow, that was a scary time, especially when I managed to get my lip caught in it! As I was getting older, the pressure to keep up my outer appearance was becoming a major fulltime job. There was not an anti-aging machine on the market that I did not own by my early forties.

The all-time worst contraption that I bought was called the micro-dermabrasion machine. It promised that it would exfoliate and suction out the wrinkles at the same time. One night, I thought the more I sucked at my wrinkles with this machine, the fewer wrinkles I would have when I woke up in the morning. I just couldn't wait to wake up with the radiant glow on my face just like the model on the cover of the box.

The next morning, I woke up with a funny sensation over my eyes. I screamed out with horror, as I looked into the mirror and found my eyes nearly swollen shut! They were literally bulging from the swelling caused by the microdermabrasion. I looked like Mohammad Ali after his worst boxing fight. It took days of icing to finally reduce the painful swelling. Afterwards, the skin around my eyes began to peel off, and left me looking like a lizard shedding its skin. This was not exactly what I had imagined based on the model's glowing skin on the cover of the box.

As if that wasn't enough torture, I had yet another machine that looked like an iron to smooth out the wrinkles on my face. I would tell my family that I just had some ironing to do as I went off into my bedroom. They had no idea what I really meant by this of course, until one day they witnessed it, and asked what the heck I was doing with an "iron" on my face. This beauty regimen took a lot of time, not to mention the monthly payments to maintain all the products that went along with it. No wonder I was exhausted and financially broke by this point. I also had a face mist machine that covered my face and made my voice sound like Darth Vader from Star Wars when I spoke through it to talk to my family. My dogs would always run and hide under the bed when I broke this gadget out from the back of the cabinet. Then finally came the nose hair trimmer incident where I almost severed my nostril off. I was just fortunate that afterwards I still had two nostrils left intact. I know that I am adding a bit of humor to these memories, but honestly, it was just sad to be held captive to my endless affairs with vanity.

My daughter was a witness to all this craziness that was locked up inside of me. Looking back, I really cannot blame her for running away from this lunacy. Most days, I wanted to run away from myself as well. Whenever I announced it was beauty night; I was like the mad scientist with nothing, but a bunch of wrinkle potions all lined up in a row. I thought to myself that if I mixed them all together at least one of them was bound to work. I fooled myself into thinking that I couldn't miss a wrinkle with this theory in mind. I didn't realize that one day this may be the sad part of my comedy act for all the women that I wanted to get out of this kind of bondage. I knew that I was not alone in my beauty regimen, and many other women were suffering under this stronghold in their lives as well.

I am so grateful that I can look back now and laugh. Thanks be to God! Nevertheless, the pain of it back then was not a joking matter. Living up to an image, that I didn't even feel worthy of having, only managed to tear my soul to pieces daily. As a woman, it is important to believe that you are beautiful both inside and out. It is the feminine dream that we all desire to have in one way or another.

As I found God's unconditional love, I began experiencing a very different type of recognition. He wanted nothing more than all my heart. His love took the years of vacant pain and insecurity away. This freedom was the beginning of unleashing the genuine beauty inside of me. I found myself no longer having shame and insecurities, but rather the faith, hope and love of a genuine woman.

As the weeks progressed, I felt deep in my spirit that God wanted me to take off my makeup and leave it off for a while. I begged him to let me keep at least some of it, but I took all my makeup off and stopped wearing it that same week. The old version of me would not have been caught dead without my makeup on. On this day however, it was His command.

107

So, I took it all off and couldn't believe how freeing it was. I wanted to jump up and yell out "this is who I really am, like it or lump it!"

God placed this indescribable genuine feeling of exquisite joy inside of my heart that made me feel more beautiful than ever. I realized that no goopy amount of makeup could have ever given me an inner beauty, such as the beauty of God's love. Despite the pressures that I had put on myself to maintain my external beauty, I finally realized the misery of why I had completely fallen apart. It was because of what I was feeling inside, which could never be hidden with makeup and external beauty.

It says in (1 Peter 3:3,4) "Do not let your adorning be external- the braiding of hair and the putting on of gold jewelry, or the clothing you wear, but let your adorning be the hidden person of the heart with the imperishable beauty of a gentle and quiet spirit, which in God's sight is very precious." These scripture verses were truly the beauty I was looking for all along, and my heart felt the deep desire to be precious in the sight of God.

Don't get me wrong, I still wore makeup, and I still wanted to look beautiful. The difference was that I no longer wanted anything ugly underneath that I had to try to hide. I was learning that genuine beauty was in the essence of a godly woman and was from the inside out. The physical manifestations in my previous appearance displayed ungodliness. Outwardly dressing up to gain attention was the telltale sign of the real story hidden underneath the years of my insecurities and the constant need to fill my ego.

I remember asking my therapist years ago why she thought I had the need to dress up this way. She told me it was an attempt to fill my ego. Well, that was the last time that I went to her for therapy because I was outright insulted, she could think such a shallow thing about me. Years later, with the help of God, I finally realized it was the truth.

Chapter 17

True Confidence

I was certain, the promise of a new future was eminent according to my faith. As it says in Jeremiah 29:11, "For I know the plans I have for you, plans to prosper you." For this reason, I refused to take another step forward with my life without God leading the way. I didn't care how long it took to finally hear the small voice inside telling me what to do next. I was left without any concrete answers as to the exact direction and purpose which my life would one day take. There wasn't anything left for me to do except to have faith in the Word to inherit God's promises (Hebrew 6:12).

My confidence was flourishing, as I furthered my relationship with God. I was finally learning who I was as a woman in the identity of Christ. After my life was turned upside down, He began turning it right side up once and for all. I started doing new things and building new habits which changed my life one step at a time. I would never have done any of this without the renewing of my mind through the sheer grace of God. My entire sense of who I was from within the deepest parts of me had begun a true transformation. It felt noticeably different than before, even if no one else thought so.

My excessive dependency on other people or looking towards worldly things for my sense of fulfillment was eliminated. I stopped comparing myself to others as the standard for my life, and instead prayed for direction. I was finished with settling for unhappiness and conforming to the normal standards of just existing. People's criticism towards me didn't seem to matter anymore. Instead, I began recognizing and focusing on my God given strengths and abilities.

In this stage of my journey, I believed that my primary focus was to seek the wisdom that God provided throughout the Bible. Catching the essence of living in God's image was truly satisfying the emptiness inside of me. Each day, I was preparing myself with the hope of a brighter future. I knew deep within me that I was already changing, as God was molding my mind into his image.

Being spiritually led meant that I no longer relied on my own insight or understanding. This was entirely different than just making my own decisions for my life based on worldly perspectives. I knew the Holy Spirit would enlighten me for a new direction. For this reason, I was able to substantiate the need for my continued faith and guidance. I was trusting and believing in God for everything I needed to find my true self.

My faith gave me a reason to wake up each day with new perspectives and the proper attitude. I was able to accept that I still had the responsibility to somehow fulfill my role as a wife and a mother. However, my identity and happiness could no longer rely solely upon these roles for my entire state of existence. By now, I knew that it was ultimately up to God to satisfy the deepest parts of me. I continued to meditate on the scripture in Philippians 4:19, "My God will meet all your needs according to the riches of his glory in Christ Jesus." The promise of God meeting every one of my needs was beginning to unfold.

Throughout the past, Mike would practically turn himself inside out, while striving within his own efforts, just trying to make me happy. I felt truly blessed he loved me so deeply that he tried just about everything to satisfy my emotional needs. Eventually, he realized that he could never provide whatever it was that I was searching for. He could never have fulfilled this seemingly bottomless hole inside of me. His efforts to please me only backfired in my own absence of knowing what God really desired for my life. His attempts to appease me only led to more discontent. I believed that my own dissatisfaction was something he was neglecting to do as my husband. This was how absurd my thinking became over the years, until I experienced God's insurmountable love. God uncovered that it wasn't Mike's job to fill the voids inside of me that only He could fill. His effort in trying to make me happy was preventing me from ever taking responsibility for myself. My need to have this excessive emotional support was completely draining the life out of him.

My outlook was finally changing, as I began to face the truth about my dysfunctional behaviors and saw things in a new light. My purpose and satisfaction did not rely on humanity or worldly possessions. God was becoming the solid foundation for my life, and my confidence was being rooted in His unconditional love. Step by step, He showed me that I had more capability than I ever believed possible. I felt the chains breaking and setting me free from the many things that were holding me back from having everything my heart truly desired. I realized that God was liberating me from self-protection and lack of vulnerability.

I would have only continued to live my days in the constant frustration of a discontented soul, until I took complete responsibility for my life, and fulfill everything God was calling me to do. This awareness literally woke me up out of a trance. Hallelujah, I wasn't meant to live in the drones of misery or settle for mediocrity anymore! I was meant to step up into my divine destiny and fulfill my calling. I was beginning to learn that my fulfillment in life ultimately depended on my everyday relationship with a loving God.

The unsatisfyingly busy days that once filled my life were brought to a complete halt. Without any distractions, I had no other choice than to hear the voice of God calling upon my life. My calling was to listen to Him with complete obedience, rather than run from the truth!

The newfound stillness in my life had a way of amplifying everything that was wrong inside of me. I believe that coming to the end of my rope was the only way I was willing to finally hear from God. I knew He was telling me that my old way of life was no longer the way to go. I encouraged

113

myself to forge ahead through God's supernatural comfort in the Word of God, knowing God was eventually going to change everything that didn't belong. I felt the former days of doubt and despair were finally behind me. For once in my life, I was about to make headway from the strongholds of yesterday's mistakes.

Chapter 18

Stolen Identity

Filling the lusts of the flesh was a never-ending battle for me. I denied myself of nothing when it came to worldly possessions, and yet I knew I was denying myself of having something more profound. I heard the voice of God finally cry out within me and move me into a more meaningful place. As I attended to the calling of my deeper desires, the shallow hungers of my yesterdays were left far behind.

I spent my life with many futile attempts at trying to fill the voids within me. I went to great lengths, striving after what I wanted to fill this empty space. Yet, as soon as I had what I thought that I wanted, no sooner did my flesh want something more. It became a vicious cycle in the never-ending game of always having a hunger for even more.

Today's society leads many to believe that having more worldly things is the ultimate source of happiness. I found through the process of elimination that my happiness was not about having more things, or that the grass was greener somewhere on the other side. My fulfillment was finally emanating from the inside ... living in God's will and finding His purpose for my life.

I can attest to a life of living in the flesh, and how it ruined my relationships. Let me be open enough to say that my behaviors were motivated by my own self-consumed, self-seeking, and unappreciative ways. I know this describes a picture of a horrible woman, and unfortunately, I was headed in a very scary direction. For so many years, I kept this secret part of my life hidden behind closed doors. I was not proud of how poorly I treated Mike, but I justified every hurtfully wrong decision that I made to survive.

Throughout the mentoring process, along with my own daily bible studies, I was finally able to face the wreckage of my self-absorbed behaviors. My life was a rocky road filled with ups and downs, which made it impossible to maintain stable relationships with myself or anyone else. For once, I was finally facing the truth by meditating on the Word of God and facing my problems. I will admit that facing it all was an extremely overwhelming feeling. However, I knew on the other side there was a more peaceful way of living. As I began understanding the process of sanctification, I was able to reflect upon all the areas of my life that fell short of the mark. I was about to venture into a new place of holiness, rather than the old worldly kind of happiness.

One such area in need of repair was my respect and use of money. Over-spending was one of the major underlying problems in my life that needed change. It not only affected me, but also my relationship with Mike. Many years ago, when it came to using credit cards, I started off on the wrong foot. I used them mindlessly, charging them up to the maximum. None of the charges were within my budget. Regardless, I bought what my flesh hungered for whenever I wanted to. There was no limit to the amounts of charges, and I basically crashed my credit by the time I was only twenty years old.

I had zero self-control in this area of my life. It took me years to rebuild my credit, and it didn't take long before I went back to abusing it all over again. Logically, I knew better than to continue with this bad habit. Yet, it seemed I still couldn't control myself. The battle was still in me, and almost anything would trigger this bad habit of always wanting more. Shopping gave me a fake sense of identity that at least made me feel like someone important. I felt powerful and in control, buying whatever it was that I wanted. I pretended that I had enough money to do whatever I wanted, as if this was the dream life. Each month, the dream came temporarily crashing down when Mike confronted me with the credit card bills.

I stayed physically fit, and whatever outfit I tried on always seemed to look so cute on me. You know how women love to say "OHHHHH this looks so CUUUUTE!" Well, that was my line way too many times. Unfortunately, I was greatly deceived by this fake sense of identity and the control it had over me. It somehow covered the constant sense of emptiness inside of me. I dressed myself all up to make it look like I had a desirable lifestyle, when really it was crumbling apart, every time I rang the credit card up, and couldn't pay it off.

I became an expert shopper. I chose what I thought was the best look for me at the time. It didn't hurt that I loved the compliments the saleswomen gave me. They were my cheerleaders; they were the ones that understood my desires. My navigation system in any store was like a trained hunting dog looking for the hidden goods. Whether there was a sale or not, I found myself circling around the clothes, nearly salivating at the thought of having MORE of them.

The saleswomen and I were always humming together in perfect harmony like "OOOOOOH and WOWWW." This was just another way of fooling myself with their guiltless approval and justifying more credit card debt to buy some more of those cute clothes. I wound up becoming very friendly with all the saleswomen. When I walked into the store, the recognition they gave me felt great! They were more than likely only smiling at me because they already knew the commission, they were about to make off me alone. It was probably like a winning lottery ticket for them because we are talking about a spending habit of thousands of dollars in clothing alone. The debt didn't matter to me because of the indescribable rush that I got from these shopping excursions. It was an addiction that I had no control over, and I went to every effort to hide this way of life from Mike. I spent his hard-working money with credit cards he didn't even know about, all to uphold my secret addiction.

I continued along this path by lying to myself that my credit card debt was not completely out of control. I strategically planned out ahead of time which credit card that I would use next by selecting the one with the lowest balance. I bounced back and forth from credit card to credit card, only fooling myself that my addiction for more "things" was not that bad. I found myself running around in circles month after month trying to pay off all the debts. It finally occurred to me that I might have a major problem. The financial path of destruction not only depleted my bank account, but eventually it depleted my state of soul, and my relationship with Mike.

At the all-time worst point in my life, I found myself charging at a rate faster than I could pay off any of the debts. I was buying clothes faster than I could wear any of them within any given season. I hadn't any room left in my closets. They were packed with tons of unworn clothes with the tags still on them. This is where it began to briefly cross my mind that maybe I might have a really, bad habit. I can recall cleaning out all my closets, astonished that I spent most of my days buying all these unnecessary things. I was finally beginning to realize that the enormous accumulation of clothes inside my closet wasn't nearly filling the empty space inside of me. The clothes that hung so lifelessly, appeared to be the skeletons in my closet.

This may sound a bit funny, but suddenly I was ready to come "out of the closet" and face the years of denial about just how many pairs of shoes that I owned. One day, I felt God urge me to spread out all my shoes on the floor, and I sat frozen for a moment in sheer disgust at my behavior. I thought to myself, "I have closets chuck full of clothes and shoes enough for an army but have only one body and a pair of feet to wear them." "What do I need all of this for?" I mean honestly on most days, I just slipped on a pair of sweatpants and flip flops, never wearing half of the things I bought anyway. I was beginning to come to my senses!

As I looked around my bedroom with complete honesty about what I was doing, I realized that I had acquired enough clothes to fill up three full length closets which were 10 feet wide, a large dresser, two end tables, half of my basement filled with storage bins, storage under my bed, and two additional ten-foot closets filled with shoes. I was a hoarder!

In our vacation home, there were yet more of my clothes. I had a walk-in-closet that was the size of a room, a large dresser, two smaller dressers, and bins of clothing there as well. Need I say more? The ironic thing is that I made sure my second home had more closets than one could ever hope to fill, and yet, I managed to fill them up anyway. Thankfully, I didn't have a third home to keep going like this.

After I became grossly aware of this bad spending habit, I began giving clothes away to the needy in attempt to justify my addiction for clothes. Although I had good intentions, I gave them away and only ended up buying more. I was only half committed to what God really wanted me to do, which was to STOP creating debt to fill my voids! During this time, I was led to a scripture that spoke out to my situation on a deep level and it said to "Keep out of debt and owe no man anything, except to love one another" (Romans 14:8).

Although these words may sound simple, the power in them sunk right into the core of me. There are so many people out there starving, homeless, and in need of clothes! Here I was spending more money on things that I didn't even need, hoping that as I filled my closets, I'd somehow fill the endless hole deep down in my gut. I suddenly realized that I was more worried about where to house my clothing, rather than considering housing for the homeless. What a wake-up call this was for me!

Sadly, it was over a twenty-year period that my insatiable thirst for shopping continued, until I was finally ready to face the reality of my compulsive spending habit. As I continued to meditate on scripture, my spirit was awakened to the truth. I finally woke up and had enough of running around in circles! I took out every single credit card in my wallet and shredded them all. I was done with waking up in the midnight hours, struck with the fear of how to pay off debt, how to keep lying while keeping secrets, and continually doing what Mike had pleaded with me not to do. For certain, it was God bringing me the truth to help me in the process of finding my identity.

Chapter 19

Vicious Cycles

As I was approaching the age of forty, I was going through the roughest point of my life. Although everything was seemingly great on the outside, my heart felt like it was completely vacant on the inside. Mike was very aware of my unhappiness and tried many things to help me, but nothing seemed to help. I was at a complete loss in my life.

Not knowing what else to do, he tried to appease me with the "things" he felt would make me happy. This being the case, he knew that I had a dream of one day owning a Mercedes sports car with a convertible rooftop. So, for that Christmas, he planned a surprise for me. His efforts were tireless, he'd go to great lengths at trying to please me.

It was early one Christmas morning. My family watched with excitement, as I drew back the curtains from the window. As I looked out the window, I thought I was seeing a mirage. There was a shiny new car parked in the driveway with a giant red bow on it! I asked my family if I was seeing things, because it seemed there was a brand-new Mercedes Benz parked in our driveway. Mike slowly walked over to me and handed me my Christmas stocking. In it was a key with a Mercedes Benz emblem on the front. I screamed out with complete surprise as I wrapped my arms around him tightly. This was it, everything I was dreaming of all wrapped up in a giant red bow!

We all ran outside together, as the sheer excitement went throughout my entire body. I stood in amazement, marveling at this gorgeous car in the driveway. I couldn't believe it was mine! The great lengths he went to secretly buy this car for me were completely unbelievable. He hid the car away for a month in his mother's garage, and brought it home late on Christmas Eve, while I was sleeping.

I sat in the car and played with all the gadgets for a while. Then I started her up and drove around town. It was only thirty-two degrees outside, and with the convertible top down it felt more like thirty below. It didn't help that I only had my flannel pajamas on (you know the cute pajamas with the built-in slippers). Anyway, I cruised around town with a giant smile on my face, as if I had just won the lottery, but in only a short matter of time the excitement of the surprise simmered down.

I began noticing that I was having this vacant feeling deep down inside myself. I knew something still wasn't right. I can't explain it, other than knowing that something major was missing in the thrill of it all. As I stood gazing at this beautiful dream car, I just couldn't seem to understand why I had felt this sense of ungratefulness. Then something powerful spoke out from the depths of my soul. I realized that buying more things was just buying me more time to continue denying whatever it was that I was really missing deep down inside.

He was willing to go to any extent to provide me with happiness. Truthfully, I eventually learned that no one could buy or create anyone else's happiness. I was completely deceived believing that it was his job to make sure I was happy in the endless cycle of having more things. My desire for material possessions to reach happiness wound up creating an extreme amount of pressure and tension within our relationship.

Although I had fun driving my dream car around town for a few minutes, I felt something deep within my spirit stirring. This led me to realize that I needed to finally let go of my long-held notion that this dream car was a way of having any joy whatsoever. I now knew that having this car fell completely short of satisfying the unmet needs inside my soul. God revealed to me that to finally get to the root cause of this uneasy feeling inside, I had to stop trying to appease myself with these momentary fixes. Three years later, I was not the least bit phased when I decided to let go of this dream car. I knew there had to be a more promising plan for my future than to cruise around town like I was the luckiest woman on earth.

When we returned the Mercedes to the dealership, the salesman asked what kind of a car we were interested in purchasing next. Mike told him that we already bought a new Jeep. The salesman's jaw dropped, and with a snooty look on his face, he acted as if we had just completely lost our minds. Honestly, I never felt more at peace in my entire life. I was finally set free from the enslavement of having to own a pretentious car, just to try and prove my own sense of self-importance.

I spent nearly half of my life dreaming of one day owning a Mercedes Benz, and suddenly it seemed completely insignificant to me. By now, the extravagances in my life were no longer my top priority. The desire to have material things became trivial in my life in comparison to the inner changes that God was offering me. During this time, God revealed that these superficial patterns were one of my major downfalls in my life. For some reason, having more money equated to being more loved in my mind, and that is why it never satisfied me on any level.

Keeping this in mind, I thought back to a time some years ago. Mike and I had this grand vision of building a dream home far away from the usual mundane way of life. During our camping vacations, we would sit underneath the stars and dream of what it would be like to have a vacation home (instead of a dirty tent). With this dream rising in our hearts, we sacrificed having many things, and finally saved enough money to make this dream come true. We watched as our dreams came to life within the process of building our new home.

At first, we were able to enjoy our dream home. It was perfectly placed amongst the mountainside in its natural surroundings. As the winter months began setting in, the bareness of the woods, and a silhouette of the mountain ridge became a place of tranquility. When daylight turned to dusk, the sky's illumination met with the warmth of its acquainted

125

sunset. We were hoping more good things were on the horizon, and this dream come true home would bring us the happiness we were both after.

There was a season for everything in this close-knit mountain community. The winter offered its finely groomed ski trails, which overlooked the peaks of mountain tops. The early spring was a time of renewal for everything in bloom, including the birth of the baby fawns. Just steps away from our backyard were plenty of hiking trails, surrounded with the privately owned game lands and views of the foliage. The summer months held onto the warmth of a private lake with beach front views, and the seclusion of this small community allowed the imagination to run off into the peaceful settings of comfort.

There we were, finally in the prime of our lives, with so many new and exciting things happening. We had finally attained the lifestyle of our dreams. This was the opportunity of a lifetime to enjoy what I believed were the finer things in life. We managed to fool ourselves for quite some time that we were having the time of our lives, but I realized deep down inside that I still was feeling unhappy. It wasn't long after settling into our dream home that my discontentment reared its ugly head and escalated into a whirlwind of negative emotions. Once again, our marriage began suffering and led us into what was an apparent disconnection.

Over the years, this dream house began to feel completely vacant. I was left feeling nothing more than guilt and condemnation. I thought repeatedly, "What is wrong with me?" I was FINALLY living the perfect life amongst my so-called dreams and desires. Yet, I was still left with this aching from an emptiness somewhere deep inside of me.

My discontentment was becoming a vicious cycle in my life. The pattern of always being in a deficit mode managed to drain Mike completely. I lived from the highs of these momentary fixes to the lows of a woman who he was unable to satisfy. My so called "perfect life" finally was about to hit rock-bottom.

Chapter 20

Stinking Thinking

I was completely unaware that I was a constant victim of my own thoughts. My negative perspectives were tearing my life and relationships apart. My imagination played out my own negative life scenarios each day. This battlefield in my mind needed a serious peace treaty. I couldn't live with hearing my own thoughts anymore!

As I became aware of this problem, I started to monitor the thoughts that I was entertaining daily. I realized something very profound, and I couldn't help but notice that there was a HUGE difference in my own thoughts versus the thoughts that God wanted for me. I had become completely aware that my own thoughts were the major reason my life was going downhill quickly. The things I kept telling myself over the course of my life were my only belief system to live or die by. As I continued to hone-in on my thoughts, I became consciously aware that I wasn't about to have any victory in my life with this negative and anxious kind of thinking.

When I focused in more on my own thoughts, I saw that they were only exaggerating negative things about Mike, and I learned that whatever negative things I was hyper-focused on about him were becoming my own reality! I believed whatever I allowed to arise in my mind, and it was destroying us. As I continued meditating on scriptures, I realized they held the practical solutions to change the way I was thinking and ensured me of a successful outcome. I eventually had to ask myself, "Why was I so focused on destroying my marriage?" For some strange reason, Mike had become a target.

The Bible had thousands of promises that were helping me to practice my faith to overcome every obstacle that I faced. The eternal Word of God became a treasure within me. I spent years aimlessly searching everywhere else in the world for the truth- all to no avail. I couldn't even begin to fathom that God's Word held the unequivocal answers to all that was seemingly a mystery to me before. I held onto them as a precious gift, knowing they were more powerful than life itself.

I began reading many of God's promises on healing and began using my faith to heal a serious health issue that I was having from the stress and anxiety. During the toughest point of my life, I began having serious problems with my stomach. The only way I can describe what it felt like was a sensation of my stomach turning itself inside out and tied into a ball of giant knots. Most days felt like a complete war zone inside of me. I could hardly eat anything because it was nearly impossible for me to swallow my food.

My esophagus felt as if it were constricted and was so inflamed that I couldn't swallow properly. It felt as if something was choking me, and I was having trouble breathing. I also had acid reflux and was popping Tums all

129

day long. My stomach literally became a burning inferno! As I was dealing with this debilitating health issue, the disappearance of my daughter had only added to the raging inferno inside of my stomach.

The years of stress in my life had finally taken its toll on me. For over two years, the symptoms from this health issue continued to hinder me. I knew that Jesus had many promises in the scriptures, which had the power to heal all our sickness and diseases. As it says in Psalm 103:2- 3, "Praise the Lord, my soul, and forget not all His benefits. He who forgives all your sins and heals all your diseases." These were the promises I was intent on having, and I was determined to find out what it would take to receive my healing. Throughout much prayer, God revealed that unless I learned to listen to His Word faithfully, I would only continue to live in the despair of my own negative thinking.

I became aware of the root cause of my sickness and was certain it was the result of my "STINKING THINKING." I had reaped from what I sowed within my own wrought up and anxious thoughts. My thoughts were literally destroying everything in my life.

I continued researching scriptures on health and healing as my only source of treatment. I knew God had promised me personally that he would heal me of this. I meditated on healing verses and read them out loud daily as my healing medicine. I came across a scripture in Proverbs 4:20-22 that struck a chord inside of me because it revealed the solution to my personal healing. It says "Attend to my words, consent and submit to my sayings. Let them not depart from your sight. Keep them at the center of your heart. They are life to those that find them, healing, and health to all their flesh."

God said to me in this promise that I needed to attend to His WORDS and not my own. His Words in these verses were my provision for God's healing over my sickness. I knew the Word of God was powerful, alive, and active. I believed wholeheartedly that God was choosing to heal me.

It also says in Isaiah 55:8, "For my thoughts are not your thoughts, neither are your ways my ways." This was not just the power of having my own "gung-ho" type of positive thinking. The result of my healing would only come from the power of my faith in God. Positive thinking relies only on one's own words, thoughts, and resources, without having the knowledge of truth.

God's Word also taught me how to gain control over my anxious thoughts, as it says in Philippians 4:6, "Do not fret or have any anxiety about anything, but in every circumstance and in everything by prayer and petition with thanksgiving continue to make your wants known to God."

As my thoughts began transforming with the Word of God, I began the healing process. Over the months, my health issue was becoming a thing of the past. As my anxious and negatively dark thoughts began unraveling, I came to the knowledge of truth. By this point, I had lost nearly 20 pounds on an already very thin physique. I weighed less than I did since I was a teenager, but I got through it just as God promised. My health was restored and my new attitude towards Mike was beginning to change things.

Chapter 21

Don't Panic

I was still having my own personal challenges, which may very well explain my lack of passion over the past few years, but as I continued to sift through the mountain of lies about how I should be living my life, all the pieces were beginning to come together. Every day, I was grasping an even deeper understanding as to why I wound up completely lost and broken.

It took time to delve into the ugliness of my broken past, and at times it knocked me completely off my feet. Even though the past was the past, the weight of having to face my sins had the power to wipe me out for days at a time. I was drained and pleaded with God to please get me to the finish line ... to let my life be completely free of the past! I knew that my healing wouldn't be complete if I didn't fully grasp the reasons for all my troubles. I had to delve into all the areas of my life, and the delusional reasons for my suffering.

I realized that I had many fears, anxieties, and overwhelming insecurities. It was at the early age of five that I could recall fear overtaking me. I was imprisoned within this worrisome life for as long as I lived before, I came to Christ. My anxieties grew into full blown panic attacks, and the fear of having the next one. It seemed like they came out of

133

nowhere. As they crept up on me, my heart would suddenly start racing and pounding at an unbearably fast rate. I felt as if it was going to pound right out of my chest and start running a marathon without me. Every time I had the shocking surge of this panic inside of me, I thought I was literally going to die from heart failure.

I was depressed, and felt helpless, as they began controlling my life with an even more unbearably paralyzing level of fear. With a heavy spirit, I forged through my days fighting this constant feeling of fearful anxiety and could not seem to identify the reasons for it. I was always left tired and worn out. My insecurities only grew as each year of my life passed. The fears began spreading like a disease throughout my life. Eventually, I was unable to live without the fear of doing anything, including the simplest of things. This paralyzing state of fear was taking over, and eventually it stopped me from practically living my life at all.

The more that I avoided doing most anything in my life, the smaller my world became. The walls felt as if they were closing in on me. This was a time when claustrophobia kicked in and began suffocating the life out of me. As I made every attempt to control my fears, I only suffered with them even more. I found that I couldn't go into small places like elevators or planes, and I could only sit in aisle seats in a room filled with people. I couldn't be pinned between people without a sudden feeling of panic. I always sat near the giant exit signs in buildings, and often needed to step outside just to gasp air back into my lungs. The truth was that I just needed to find some sort of an escape from the fears living inside of me. Running from them was my usual and ordinary "go to" for personal consolation.

Satan used fear as a roadblock to keep me from ever living in God's plan. The enemy smelled my fears like a shark smelled blood in water. I felt like a caged animal pacing back and forth, just contemplating ways to break free from the feeling of confinement. There was never any freedom living in my own prison of fears, but my walk of faith was not about me taking matters into my own hands anymore. I knew that with my faith, I was no longer alone. I was being led into something greater, as the Lord promised to help me overcome my fears and anxieties.

I was ready to fight this battle of angst ... and then there came a day I will never forget. It was the final battle against panic and anxiety. As this episode of anxiety began, my heart nearly pounded out of my chest, but this time I was intent on overcoming the panic! I finally had enough of living under this evil curse that plagued me for so many years of my life. It took complete faith and authority to stand up to the enemy once and for all. I knew that I finally had the power within me to resist the enemy's lies about fear.

It was in the confines of my bedroom when I fiercely screamed out the Word of God, faithfully professing it over the anxiety! I got angry with the hungry beast looking to devour my soul. I believe that an exorcism of some sort had taken place, except my head didn't spin around in a 360 on my shoulders. I continued to yell out the Word of God and

135

meant every word that I said to chase that demon away for good. Mike had overheard me in the bedroom grunting at this evil spirit in me and innately knew that he needed to leave as quickly as he could.

I suddenly found myself on the floor beside the bed on my knees, wondering for a second if this was the last breath I would ever take, only to find myself punching myself in the stomach and yelling at the demons to, "GET OUT!" It was like an outer body experience, as I saw myself punching my stomach and wondered what I was doing. Suddenly, it stopped. It was gone! I felt the spirit of panic and fear leave my body, and I knew that I had won. I fell back into bed and laid there exhausted for a while, knowing something that did not belong had left my body for good. My life miraculously changed from that day forward! After thirty-four years of suffering with severe anxiety episodes, I never had another panic attack again.

I noticed that I was free of fear and went into elevators without a second thought, and purposely sat in the center aisles without any fears. I no longer woke up in the middle of the night with my heart racing. After so many years of fearing that my heart would start beating out of control, I found an inner peace and calmness like I never had known before. The spirit of fear that had kept my body in a complete state of panic was finally gone for good. There was certainly no rational explanation as to what had taken place that day in the natural realm. It was a surreal experience of God performing a sheer miracle of healing in my life.

Chapter 22

Bittersweet

Over time, I was able to ponder the long list of reasons as to why my heart had grown cold (especially in my marriage). I focused on Mike's faults and held onto the bitter grudges of yesterday's mistakes. We were always at odds because of our difference of opinions. I insisted upon the need to always be right. This turned me into a wife with the sharp edge of a rebellious personality.

For the first time, I faced the convictions of God head on about my behaviors. For once in my life, I needed to STOP blaming Mike for the problems we were facing. The personal extent of my problems was because of my own broken-down state of soul that had deteriorated from my negative mindset.

The years of my negative thoughts and behaviors allowed my bitterness to become deeply rooted in my character. All my reactions stemmed from this broken place inside of me. Eventually, it was not only my husband that I turned bitter cold on, but most of my other relationships as well. The resentment inside of me was running rampant from one relationship to the other. By this time, my perspectives were seen from a completely broken state of heart and soul.

Over the years, I believed that my only line of defense was to use a bitter reaction as my source of protection. In my eyes, everyone else was the enemy, and as my resentment accumulated, so did my account of other's faults. I was in a vulnerable place in the hands of the enemy, just waiting to devour my soul. I was fooled by a false reality, thinking nothing but negative thoughts about Mike repeatedly. By this time, my relationships weren't bearing anything except for the bitter fruits of a timeworn tree.

Slowly but surely, I became captive by the bitter thoughts, until I realized it was Satan's tactics. My negative way of thinking managed to tear me away from any love inside my heart. This ugly side of me came out more under the pressures of mentorship. All the years of resentment had festered inside of me, until the mentoring process struck the bitter chords.

My disheartened state caused me to push people out of my life and separated me from all that life made dear. My destructive behaviors were made brutally clear to me on the tragic day of my daughter's runaway. I had come face to face with my own broken state of reality in the moment I realized she was gone. Eventually, I was left feeling like a lonely outcast, locked within the walls of my own solitary confines. My heart had hardened from years of toxic thoughts, and my perspectives towards my relationships were completely contaminated.

Seeing through the eyes of bitterness only made me that much angrier. My reactions were always snappy and did nothing more than lead us to family disputes. I majored in the minor details of any situation. Eventually, I had all the ammunition I needed to explode over virtually nothing at all. The battles inside of me were causing us all broken hearts and great loss.

The conflicts in my relationships were all around me like a war zone. This battlefield ultimately left me alone with the realization that the conflict was not around me, but rather was within me. My mind, will, and emotions were fighting against God's will for my life. The longer that I ignored my inner battles, the deeper I fell into wickedness. Eventually, my entire world became the shattered remains of my own poisoned state of soul.

After nearly a year of reflecting on my own state of being, I was brought to a place of humility, and began to become free from the strongholds of bitterness and resentment. I surrounded myself with God's truth to practically guide me in a new direction to mend my relationships. I came to my senses, realizing it wasn't everyone else that was always the problem. As I unraveled the bitter cords tangled up inside of me, I wanted nothing more than to rebuild trust in my relationships. I wanted to begin by having a better attitude and thanking God for all the good things that I could find to be grateful for about my husband.

Chapter 23

Let Her Go

After Shannon's runaway, the feeling of rejection left me in an extreme state of emotional turmoil. I desperately wanted the opportunity to mend the shattered pieces in our lives. It was apparent that she left because there were underlying issues between us that were in desperate need of resolve.

Over the months, there were only brief moments that we spoke over the phone. I felt as if motherhood was just stripped away from me. I had no idea when I would ever see her again, and the loneliness struck me to the core.

I was questioned by every person in town since the moment of her disappearance. This included the police department, detectives, family members, friends, and neighbors. I was interrogated for having this apparent estrangement between us. Suddenly, I felt the detectives alluding to the possibility of me being a suspect in the missing case of my daughter. It all felt like a bad dream that I couldn't wake up from. Around every corner was yet another surprise.

All these conversations were always followed by blank stares, deafening silence, and the look of judgment. In my attempt to avoid people's constant questioning, I became reclusive within my own home. I knew this situation reflected something that I had neglected to do. I felt completely ashamed and hopeless as a mother. I knew however, that whatever it was that I did wrong couldn't have measured up to the reasons for her betrayal in running away like she did. I spent my days hoping the pain of it all would just become an invisible thing of the past.

To survive, I kept myself submerged in the Word of God to keep on the right path of thoughts. It was literally what kept my sanity and set me free from the anguish I was suffering from. I thanked the Lord every single day for coming into my life as my Savior. I knew that without Him, I would not have made it through any of this in one piece. I would have been up against the judgment of people without God being on my side. I repeated the scripture in my head over and over in Romans 8:31, "If God is for us who can be against us?" I knew He was working behind the scenes and placing all the pieces in our lives back together again.

Shannon began contacting me over the months, mostly through her emails. This was her attempt to sort things out from a safe distance. I could see by her emails that she was pretending she hadn't a care in the world. I made a conscious decision not to lose control over my feelings about how hurtful and senseless this all seemed. In my wildest dreams, I never could have imagined this is how things would have turned out between us. Nevertheless, I knew I had no control over the path that she was on, and I knew I had no other choice than to let her go.

While she was in places that I did not even know about, I prayed relentlessly. Many nights, I woke up in a pool of cold sweat wondering if she was still really gone. Many mornings, I woke up in a so much despair that it seemed impossible to get out of bed. I spent the morning hours undoing the shock of it all by meditating on the Word of God and praying for her safe return.

I didn't know what she was getting herself into, and I will not deny that most days it took everything inside of me to keep it together and not have a breakdown. It had been many long and painful months since she was home. I endured the pain of missing her through many family events such as holidays, birthdays, vacations, and our everyday routines. As the shock of it all began to wear off, I was left with a complete sense of loss without her. Letting go seemed like a constant uphill battle.

Chapter 24

The Reunion

As the months continued, Shannon's room was left with only the echoes of silence and the desolate reminders of her runaway. I had only a dream that one day she would return to fill this empty space. Even though she was long gone, the subtle scent of her perfume remained. As I sat quietly, my mind went back to when she was just a little girl and how I tucked her into bed, knowing that as soon as the sun would rise in its usual place, she would too. I was desperate for her closeness again. I had only the memories of what we once shared in the room where she once was.

The moments of silence gave me more time to continue reflecting upon my own life. The stillness led me to remember the years I lived in the silence of unresolved emotional issues. This silent pain screamed out at me on the day of her disappearance. I desperately wanted to let go of every feeling of pain and start anew. I didn't want my daughter to come back to any of the painful reminders of the past.

Seven months had gone by since I had seen her last, and I began packing away all of what remained in her room. The memories of the past adorned her shelves and felt like a ghostly reminder of who she once was. I felt a sadness, knowing this chapter in our lives had been viciously torn away from us. It seemed as if her childhood had just vanished like the wind in the sudden drama of how it ended. Nevertheless, by now I was focused on the dreams of our future together. I wanted to wash away any memory of this tragedy and move on.

After ten long months of waiting patiently, she was finally ready, and announced she was coming back home to visit. I wanted her to know that things were no longer in a state of shambles. I was a changed woman and hoped to be a better mother. I knew her run away seemed to signify our unsolved problems, but we finally had the chance to forgive one another, and rebuild our lives. I didn't want anything, including myself, to be the same, as when she left home. I spent the months discovering all of what I felt was broken and battered inside of me. The decision to resolve my own issues was pivotal for repairing my relationship with her. Over the months, I worked not only on fixing what was broken inside of me, but also began fixing what had fallen apart around me.

The awaited day of her return finally arrived. It was June 17th, and she was due to come in on an afternoon flight. The week leading up to this point was an emotional roller coaster, with so much anticipation. I knew this visit was just a beginning in our reconciliation. I tried to keep myself calm, though my emotions were running high in this bittersweet moment. I wondered how it would be possible to make up for the lost time, knowing we only had two weeks of time together. I was beginning to feel some mixed emotions about seeing her for the first time since the runaway. I could feel my anger rising because of the unresolved issues we needed to confront together. There were no apologies yet, so the hurt and distrust were still eminent.

It was challenging for me to hold back my incredibly mixed emotions, as Mike and I arrived at the airport. I had so many questions still running through my mind. I wondered what we would even say to each other, or how I would ever prepare myself to hear her reasons for leaving home. How could I be sure that I wouldn't say anything wrong, which might drive her even further away?

I kept thinking about all these unanswered questions as my heart began pounding and palpitating. My chest began tightening, and at one point, I wondered if I was going to die from anticipation before I ever saw her again! I had to gain control over my thoughts, which were running rampant like a wild horse inside of my head. I changed these untamed thoughts by focusing on all the ways which God had come through for all of us during this trying time. I believed my faith had led us to this victorious moment of togetherness.

As Mike and I waited for her to come through the arrival gate, we held up these funny cardboard signs that I made while I was home. Written on the front of them in black bold letters were, "MOM and POP", in case she forgot who we were. I needed to break the ice and find humor in all this somewhere. So, we held up our signs like two embarrassing old fools. I knew she would get a kick out of the fact that somethings quirky about me just didn't change.

We waited for what seemed like an eternity for her plane to arrive. Fifteen minutes prior to her landing my anticipation was completely overwhelming me, and I could no longer hold back my emotions. My insides began shaking like an earthquake, and my eyes welled up with great big tears that seemed would never stop. As I wiped them away, I paced back and forth, hoping that it would ease the tension building inside of me.

As I stared at the flight arrivals screen, I anxiously waited for it to display that her plane had landed. Finally, after great anticipation, the screen registered her planes arrival. We searched desperately for her through all the people arriving from their flights. She must have wanted to make a grand entrance because every single passenger came off the plane except for her. As we stood stretching our necks, looking down the long vacant corridor, we finally saw her making her way towards us. I will never forget how she was glowing with this unforgettable smile on her face. We quickly grabbed her and embraced in a long-awaited hug. It was the moment I had dreamt of every second of each day since she left.

I took a long look at her and felt as though she had somehow grown up without me. I instantly felt my heart sadden. As we walked out of the airport I wondered, "Who was this girl?" She seemed like a stranger to me. She walked so carelessly as if it was just an ordinary day. I guess it was a

146

cover up for all the shattered pieces she had left behind. It was clear to me that we had all surrounded ourselves with this obviously nonchalant attitude for this bittersweet moment. The rawness of our emotions remained, and our hearts were guarded.

We casually walked out of the airport and spoke of the weather, as if we were just mere acquaintances. I mean honestly, what else could we possibly have said to each other? Expressing our feelings and saying words like "I love you" just didn't seem to fill our hearts in the moment. Instead, there stood an awkwardness between us.

As we drove home, our hearts only allowed for some small talk. I can't remember what we said to each other because I was feeling completely numb seeing her again. I knew so many things were still standing in our way and keeping us at a distance, but things seemed a bit more normal when we arrived home. Our dogs practically jumped out of their fur with sheer excitement once they saw her. As she embraced her brother with a horseplay kind of hug, my heart filled with the warmth of our family feeling complete again.

We could hardly wait to see her reaction when she saw the renovation of her room. We grabbed hold of her and covered up her eyes with our hands. As we uncovered them, I knew it was a great success just by the expression of joy on her face. Shortly after, she settled in and we nestled on the couch together, desperately searching for the right words to say.

Not many words were spoken. Instead, it seemed as if a giant white elephant was standing in the room. We both completely avoided the much-needed discussion about her reasons for running away. While screaming at her at the top of my lungs did briefly cross my mind, I decided that ordering take-out dinner was the next best thing to do. During the dreadful months of her absence, dinners were an especially tough time for me. Every night I had inadvertently placed a table setting where she once sat. After realizing what I did, I hesitantly removed it from the table, and stared at her empty chair. So, on this night, I was especially excited to fix her a place setting, knowing she would fill the empty space that was missing for so long.

I was looking forward to a freshly made New York pizza. She complained that California pizza was absolutely the worst, (pineapple pizza, yuck)! I knew that New York pizza would top at least something she had in California. That is how desperate I was to find anything that would please her to be back home. After dinner, we spent the evening looking at her pictures, which she had taken over the past months. They were filled with the places she had seen and the new friends she met. Instantly I felt my heart break. She acted like leaving home was this exciting adventure. It looked like she had built an entirely new life for herself, while I was left behind, just trying to survive the devastation! I bit down hard on my lip, as I continued looking through the pictures. I felt something hurtful beginning to rise inside of me and I really wanted to slap some sense into her! I asked myself repeatedly, "What in the world is she thinking?!!!" She locked us out of her life for months, and I knew nothing about her life and these so-called friends. She acted as though they were more important than her own family. It seemed to me as if she completely detached from us and replaced her family with her new friends.

I realized she wanted it to appear as if she had everything she wanted, knowing deep down how tragic it was that she had thrown everything from her past away. The blatant disrespect practically made me lose my mind, but by the grace of God, I maintained my composure, until it was time to get real with each other. I believed I had God's favor and couldn't allow her lack of compassion to lead me to say something I'd regret later.

The very next day we started communicating on a deeper level than ever before. She told me some of the reasons why she left for California. After she confided in me that her visions of being a singer/songwriter were something that she secretly desired since she was fifteen years old, I realized that I had no idea who she really was during this time. Sadly, she expressed her teenage years were a struggle for her and writing helped her through the toughest times. I thought back and wondered where I was at that time in her life. I realized that I had no clue of what my daughter was going through while growing up.

It hit me hard, truly facing the fact that I was too caught up with my own unhappiness to even have time to notice her struggles. I would rather not have reflected over these unhappy times in our lives, and yet staring me straight in the face was that period when my own destructive choices affected my entire family.

With everything weighing on my mind, I finally broke down and expressed how betrayed I felt because of her dreadful decision to run away. I was honest with my emotions, and everything came pouring out. I really didn't want to condemn her for what she had done to me, but I needed her to know that she hurt me so deeply that it was beyond anything imaginable. She needed to know the reality of the pain that I quietly suffered while she was gone.

In the middle of my crying and screaming, my eyes glanced up at her. The excruciatingly sad look on her face was something I will never forget. The heavy weight of what she had done to me had finally become her reality too. Her face and body drooped downward with the weight of everything she had done wrong. The shattered pieces of our lives left grief standing between us. There were no words of an actual apology, but the sorrow on her face said it all, and it was something that I needed to see for me to let go and really begin to forgive her. In this moment of regrets, we had no other choice but to finally face the brokenness inside both our hearts. The ugly picture of the past several months finally became clear to her, as did the wreckage that it caused both of us. It felt as if we had crossed over a major roadblock that was standing in our way. I sensed the slightest feeling of headway in our relationship, and I knew this was truly the beginning of rebuilding the broken pieces.

Before we knew it, two weeks had passed, and her visit was coming to a sudden end. Throughout the weeks, I fought the thoughts of this day from even entering my mind. Several nights before the final day of her visit, we spent the evening curled up on the couch together. As I stroked her hair, I knew I was about to face the reality of letting her go all over again. The final days of her visit passed quickly, and the morning of her departure was finally upon us. As we drove along the highway towards the airport there was not a word uttered between us. I had all I could do to keep myself from falling apart. When we finally arrived at the airport, I only wished she would have said that she wanted to come back home with us again, but deep down, I knew something in her heart was calling her back to California.

As we made our way into the airport, I could no longer deny the reality of her leaving home once again. We slowly walked towards the departure gate and hugged for a while, hoping it would never end. I knew I was already feeling the pain of missing her again. The uncertainty of when we would see one another again went through my mind, but for her sake, I held my chin up and tried desperately to be cheerful as we exchanged a few last words. We were reminiscent of the time that we spent together over the past two weeks, but as I slowly glanced over at the clock, I noticed our time together was finally up. With one final hug, I had no other choice than to let her go and say goodbye. When she turned away and headed for the terminal, it was a reminder of that day I put her on the school bus, she didn't look back again.

Chapter 25

Marital Awakening

After she returned to California, I continued to address the many things that previously went wrong within my own life. This took many reflective thoughts to understand how my life wound up in such a state of turmoil. Looking back over the past twenty years, my marriage was certainly not all I dreamt it would be. We began as most couples would have, with the highest of hopes and dreams. Unfortunately, the reality of our dreams had an abrupt ending after only the first few months of our marriage.

The overwhelming responsibilities as a newly married couple seemed to hit us square in the face. We didn't have two dimes to rub together and found ourselves already buried underneath the mortgage payments and student loans. A year into our marriage, our first baby was already on the way. Prior to my pregnancy, we managed to find an inexpensive health care coverage plan we could well afford.

After my first prenatal visit to the doctor's office, they regretfully informed me that our new insurance coverage had certain terms in its policy. Apparently, there was an initial waiting period until we were eligible for prenatal benefits. This must have been written in the very, very, VERY fine print. Being that I was pregnant before the agreed upon terms, we were told that we did not have any insurance coverage for our pregnancy. Without having any insurance coverage, our out- of-pocket cost became a total of ten thousand dollars. This was money that we did not have. Our only option was to make a payment plan with the hospital. It took five long years to pay off this debt.

Along the course of my pregnancy, I went from a size zero to what felt like the size of an extra bloated whale! Even my nose was bloated, and it spread out to the entire width of my face. By the time Halloween rolled around, I thought it was appropriate to dress up for a costume party. So, I decided to dress up as a giant orange pumpkin. As I made my grand entrance into the party, everyone's attention took me by surprise. They took one look at me and started laughing uncontrollably. There I was looking like a giant orange spectacle! Gee, I liked getting attention, but there apparent laughing and pointing at me was a bit overwhelming. As my hormones started to kick in, I suddenly felt a welling up inside of me, as if I needed to burst out and cry hysterically. I thought, "OH PLEASE NO!" I envisioned myself as a crying pumpkin and knew this could be a very embarrassing moment. Even though my eyes were welling up, I began laughing hysterically, joining the rest of the party, as I tried desperately to hold back the tears in my eyes. Throughout the entire night, I tried to avoid bumping into the skinny woman wearing the tight sexy black cat costume (there always seemed to be one of them). I sneered at her because the only thing sexy on me that night was the skinny pumpkin stem on top of my head, but it turned out that I made honorable mention as the runner up for the best costume, which wasn't a proud moment because the winner was Frankenstein.

A little over a month later, I spent thirty-two hours in a natural birthing center trying to give birth to my daughter. This was abruptly interrupted with the threat that I may have toxic shock syndrome. We drove frantically to the hospital during rush hour in a torrential downpour. Along the way, I was screaming some ugly things in the back seat of the car. I think I was gnawing on the back of the leather seat from the pain. Nothing about that day was what I dreamt it would be. After I made my grand entrance into the hospital looking like a worn-out grizzly bear, everyone was staring at me once again. I thought, "They should have seen me in my pumpkin costume if they thought I looked hideous now." I was finally admitted and immediately required a caesarian section. My daughter and I both wound up with fevers and infections. We were consequently hospitalized for days. I found no rest once we arrived home. My daughter and I were kept awake every night for the next six months with her severe colic.

Mike went off to work leaving me alone with our baby for ten to twelve hours a day. On his days off we couldn't afford to hire anyone to babysit, or to do any needed maintenance on the house. The hours alone together were few and far between. The days seemed never ending with a colicky baby crying all day and night. I was exhausted, lonely, and miserable. I was without any relief because I was stuck to my baby, breast feeding twenty-four hours a day. Before I gave birth, I thought breast feeding sounded like a naturally bonding experience. After a month, this idea didn't seem so great to me anymore. The feedings were every hour, and by this point my nipples were turning as red as Rudolph the red nosed reindeer. She was literally attached to me around the clock for one year. I didn't want to be ungrateful for her, but this was far more demanding than I had ever imagined it would be.

All along, Mike was feeling completely left out with the sudden loss of attention from me. So, he went about his busy days at work, while I went about mine at home. On the weekends his involvement with the house projects seemed to overtake his life. We usually met up on Saturday night for a romantic evening, which often ended up with us yawning in each other's faces. On Sundays, he was so exhausted from the week that he napped for most of the afternoon. My loneliness became a rude awakening even in the earliest days of my marriage. My life seemed to have turned out quite differently than I had expected. Although we did have an adorable house, healthy babies, and a shiny new car, I still felt a void somewhere deep inside of me. My marriage seemed to deny me of having a deeper inner satisfaction. I knew that I needed something more within myself. This feeling of dissatisfaction led me to believe that I wasn't happy with my marriage anymore. With my unreasonable expectations, the tension between us only escalated, and the relationship grew cold and distant. Somehow, we managed to keep it all together for the sake of our dreams, which had not yet fallen apart entirely. Over the years, our intimacy was deteriorating, and although we appeared to be the perfect couple on the outside, behind the scenes it was a completely different picture.

Chapter 26

Behind the Scenes

Over five years had passed when we finally managed to save enough money to buy a bigger house. It was in an affluent, quaint town on the North Shore of Long Island. The school district was acclaimed to be one of the most outstanding public-school systems. My so-called dreams were finally coming true with this small town being such a wonderful place to live. Our lives looked promising, and I believed we were finally moving up in the world. We had more money, a bigger house, and the well-acclaimed schools for our children. We were living amongst some of the wealthiest people in the world and becoming one of them was a dream that I could almost taste.

The greatly awaited day of moving up in the world to our new home was utterly chaotic. The moving truck broke down on the way to our house, and I waited hours for a different truck to arrive later that night. Mike couldn't take off from work because we needed every dime that he made. So, I sat all day and waited in a house filled with nothing more than empty boxes. We also rented a U-Haul truck to save money, by moving some of our own things later that evening. After finally arriving in our new hometown, we unloaded everything from the U-Haul truck. Somehow, this wasn't exactly what I dreamed of when I thought of this day.

Well into the wee hours of the night, we unloaded our things from the truck. We spent the night running a fifty-yard dash with heavy boxes in our arms. I unpacked all the boxes over the next few weeks, and we settled in for all of what was about to unfold in our lives over the next ten years.

A year later, out of nowhere, I suffered with a debilitating vertigo attack. I couldn't see straight, and I could barely walk. The severity of this went on for years with no known cure. I continued to suffer with it somewhat less intensely over the years of my life. I had no help with the daily routine of raising my kids and suffered through this time with extreme dizziness. The stressful years went on and before we knew it, the children were growing older. The feeling of disconnect between Mike and I was at an all-time high. His overly busy life wore us down and tore us apart. However, with the kids growing older and becoming less demanding, I decided to help in my husband's office. His office had the convenience of being right in our own home, so I could oversee the kids too. I managed his office for the next five years, until I realized that I had enough. I felt like it was time for a change in my life, so I hired a new office manager to replace me. It seemed that there was something else that was calling out to me, and yet, I still didn't know what it was that I really desired to do with my life. After I resigned from his office, the division in our lives became progressively worse over the years.

His business seemed to consume him, and eventually my resentment towards him, eroded the intimacy in our relationship. He was an extremely driven man, and there was no force that was ever going to stop him from accomplishing everything that he had his sights on. Unfortunately, by this point, I believed that his sights were no longer on me. Over the years, I grew painstakingly lonely. I didn't want to complain because I knew that he was a hardworking man. I knew how driven he was when I married him, and I knew that would provide for our family. The truth was that even though I knew I had a void in my own personal life, I couldn't deny feeling unhappy with the dynamics of our marriage by this point either. Our lives didn't seem to be compatible with each other anymore.

The guilt that I endured about my unhappiness never allowed for my freedom to communicate honestly. The freedom from my misery in the marriage seemed impossible. I felt stuck within the confinements of a lonely marriage and the responsibility of two young children. Some years had passed, and I tried to make the best of whatever moments we had together, but my thoughts of resentment were pouring out of my soul like wildfire. By this time, I found myself feeling utterly lost in my life. The thought of my children growing older scared me like nothing ever had before. The loneliest thought that I could have ever imagined was to be left alone in my marriage after my children were gone.

Without overly demanding children anymore, I began turning my attention to myself. I decided to give myself a new sense of inspiration by losing weight and working out more often. I realized deep down inside that nothing about my life was right anymore and tried desperately to fix it. Most of my emotional, physical, and spiritual needs were left on the side lines for far too long. Since no one else seemed able to meet my needs, I began recklessly trying to fill them myself. In the attempts to find out what I was meant to do with my life, I thought I had no other choice than to follow my own heart and this was the beginning of my deepest and darkest troubles.

My self-pity began causing even more resentful thoughts than ever before. I began turning more inwards to my self-wallowing thoughts. No one else seemed to matter anymore except for me. Before I knew it, my emotions threw my world around into a never-ending tailspin. I allowed my every negative emotion to dictate my life. My bitter soul was filled with hatred because I regretted that my life did not turn out as I dreamed it would. My life began flashing before me, and I saw my dreams quickly crashing in all around me. Everything seemed to spiral completely out of control. In one final swoop, I gave up on myself and my marriage. It was the decision that made something deep inside of me just snap. Everything about me began changing for the worse. This was the tipping point which I believe led to my destruction. Without a doubt, something overtook me, and my evil pursuits took off like rapid wildfire. I was energized by the power of wickedness. I was emotionally and physically on the run in an altered state, trying to entice other men promising pleasure and ecstasy, but only delivered death and shame. I had indeed become the strange, flattering, dangerous woman found in Proverbs 2:16.

The next thing I knew, I was flaunting my sexuality in a way that was odious to God. I was parading around in tight and skimpy clothing, looking like a prostitute- and causing other men to stumble into visual heart-level adultery. I began pursuing and luring in my lovers with a fierce vengeance to destroy my life. I began to carry out my hidden plans approximately one year later. I found myself falling into the arms of Mr. Wrong, wanting desperately to feel alive again. My wicked desire for sexual attention only escalated because of its failure to truly satisfy me. At one point, I wished that Mike had caught me in the act of the illicit affair, just as an easy way out of our marriage. The guilt from the affair was killing me, and of course, I blamed that on Mike too. I wanted out of this life, and in the background of my mind, suicide became a distant thought.

I can remember feeling justified in the pursuit of other men because of Mike's neglect to cherish me exactly the way that I wanted. I realized later how impossible that would have been because my hateful words and actions only pushed him further away. My insatiable secret desires only drove him even further away. Over this painful time, I realized that I wasn't honest with myself or anyone around me. I had no idea who I was anymore, and the affair ended with an excruciatingly painful loss of something deep inside. The extent of damage done to myself, and my family, was a complete disgrace.

As I ended the affair, the sudden loss of attention left me feeling even more broken and desperate than ever. Before I could even allow myself to feel the entire extent of the pain from what I had done, I suddenly found myself pursuing other lovers. I was once again, lost in the act of another affair, but my loneliness only grew in leaps and bounds. I was more lost than ever and could not find my way out. Deep down, I knew that I was never meant to be with either one of these lost men, but during that time my utter state of brokenness outweighed any rational behavior to deter me from being an adulterous woman. I didn't seem to care about whether it was right or wrong if I had someone's attention.

When the acts of the sexual affairs quickly faded, I was left with a gnawing pain inside my soul. The despair began pushing me into a deep depression, and I hit an all-time low. It left me in the depths of an emotionally paralyzed state, and I knew that I had come to the end of my rope. I felt trapped in a corner and could no longer keep running. Rock bottom had become the defining moment when God came into my life, unlike ever before. I began praying for a way out of this horrible place in my life and noticed an unexplainable strength that I couldn't seem to find before. This was the turning point, where I knew I had to rely on God for the inner strength to overcome the craving for sexual attention and break the cycle of addiction.

Chapter 27

The Confession

I questioned myself for years over my dissatisfaction in my marriage. Yet, I had seen so many other marriages that didn't have half as much love as ours (which wasn't much). According to God's image of a covenant marriage, comparing what I had to most anyone else's was setting a low standard for the basis of my own marital relationship. Over the years, I became increasingly more aware that I was always longing for something that I thought wasn't fulfilling me in my marriage. At times, I believed that maybe it was because I was meant to be married to someone else (more perfect than Mike was). No matter what I did, I just could not seem to shake this inner voice telling me there was someone else out there that was meant for me.

Without the knowledge of truth, the only direction that I had left was to live out Satan's plan to destroy me and my family with the affairs. This was an extremely vulnerable time for me, and I was prey for the evil predator while in the depths of my own despair. Satan was trying to destroy me and my life in one final swoop. I didn't have any answers as to why I felt so empty and distraught all the time. My morals flew out the window, and I cracked under the pressure of not having this inner source of fulfillment that I was searching for.

If I had known God prior to my troubles and infidelity, I knew that I would never have chosen to sell my soul by secretly planning and carrying out the illicit affairs. I am not excusing myself from them because anyone knows that fidelity is expected with the bond of a marriage. I write from where I am now looking back, and I know that the old me was convinced that I didn't have any other choice. I was desperate, and Satan's deception slowly convinced me that I was a worthless woman.

I listened to these lies in my head over and over and didn't value most anything in my life anymore. I knew better than to carry on with the affairs while I was a married woman with two children. I spent a lot of time wondering why I would do such a terribly irresponsible thing, but at the time, the voids in my life overruled, and I had no true shame for my actions. I was without any knowing of who I truly was as a woman, or what kind of life that I wanted anymore.

I didn't understand why I couldn't have pulled myself away from my miserable life of sins, until I read the passages describing my dilemma in (Romans 7:15), "I do not understand what I do. For what I want to do, I do not do, but what I hate to do." Also, in Romans 7:18-20, "I have the desire to do what is good, but I cannot carry it out. I do not do the good I want to, but the evil I do not want to- this I keep on doing. Now if I do what I do not want to do, it is no longer I who did it, but it is the sin living in me that does it." When I read these verses, I realized at the time that I was fighting against another kind of spirit that had taken root within me, but over time, and with much struggle, I finally faced the truth about what led to my sinful ways.

As I began turning this corner in my life, I was faced with the utter state of destruction in my marriage. I could not go on another day without confessing my secret life of sin to Mike. I was petrified to tell him what I had done. I thought about what kind of explosive reaction he might have. I was truly sorry for committing these sins, and I wished that I could go back in time and erase everything that I did, except I couldn't. I wanted a chance to be honest, and apologize to Mike, in the hopes of rebuilding the trust in our relationship.

I felt God leading me to confess all of it to him, no matter how scared I was to tell him what I did. I have never been so ashamed in my life and trying to find the right words to say seemed impossible, except for, "I am truly sorry that I did this and hurt you so deeply." He was shocked, enraged, hurt, angry, and never in his wildest dreams had thought that I would do anything like this ... he trusted me, and I shattered our lives to pieces. There are no words to describe what a dreadfully painful day it was to confess the truth to him.

He had to walk away from me and be alone for a while, but when he was done praying silently, he came back into the room where I was, and while he began yelling at me, his pale face turned to deep shades of purple and red. As he sat in the chair across from me, his veins began popping out of his neck, and suddenly he screamed out, "How could you do this?!!!" "What were you thinking?!!!" I stared at him silently and had no excuses for myself, and yet was not

165

prepared for what was about to happen next, as the questions from him came rolling in like a tidal wave. I did not see any this coming and I tried to answer his questions as best as I could, but the more he questioned me, the worse I felt. I knew that nothing I was saying made any sense to him. There was no way that he could've understood the living hell I was stuck in, and how it spiraled out of my control at the time. It was all completely unexplainable, even to me.

I took full responsibility for my actions and promised him that the affairs were over for years by this point, and this would never happen again. I had planned on him never knowing about my secret life. I was going to take it to my grave, until I realized I was not being totally honest, and he deserved to know the truth. He deserved to know why I was emotionally and physically vacant for the past several years. He deserved to know why I had left his life, and he deserved to know where his wife had been.

For me, the past several years was a complete blur. It was difficult to remember time frames, and all the dishonest things that I had blocked out of my mind were all coming back. Still, there was a sense of relief for both of us that the secrets were no longer standing between us. They were all out on the table, and I had come to the plate, willing to humble myself and prove my love for him if he would be gracious enough to forgive me and give me another chance.

Chapter 28

The Restoration Process

Only several days after I confessed the truth to Mike about the affairs, he came over to me and held me tight. He said, "Confessing the truth to me about the affairs was the right thing to do." "I feel like we have removed a huge problem that was standing between us." We can heal from this together and finally have the kind of marriage we've always dreamed of from the beginning." I was completely taken back that he responded so quickly and had the grace to forgive me! It seemed that our future was going to be filled with everything we had ever desired.

There was a long road ahead of us, but this had to be a personal journey that restored my wholeness. God pulled me out from the living Hell of being an adulterous wife, and it was time to restore the broken parts of my soul. Although the affairs were long over, my nightmares still weren't.

After the whirlwind from this storm in our lives had finally settled down, rebuilding the broken pieces of our marriage wouldn't be easy. The hurt was still raw despite the forgiveness. I was finally reaping the consequences of my own betrayal, as it swung around like a boomerang. I also knew that my daughter's betrayal in running away was a spirit that was led by my own. Her runaway was one of the most tragic moments of my life because I realized her spirit mirrored my own image. I was left with the regrets that tore apart my family. Healing for all of us would not be easy.

On the day of my confession, and in the months that followed my daughter's runaway, my mind was still screaming from the guilt of the affairs. I knew they played a crucial part in the result of our lives being torn apart. My secrets ate away at me day in and day out. I was unable to move past the reasons for these tragic events. I played out the affairs repeatedly in my mind. I condemned myself until the torment of it was overwhelmingly unbearable. Eventually, I finally had enough of beating myself up for what I had done and began the healing process that God was offering me.

Every part of this journey, there was a process of repenting of my past sins. This led the way for my own healing to begin. Meditating on God's Word and knowing that I had the Lord's forgiveness was the final piece to be able to move forward. Letting go of the shame over what I had done was only possible for me because I finally knew that God was full of His mercy and forgiveness. I found comfort and reassurance in Romans 4:7, "Blessed and happy and to be envied are those whose iniquities are forgiven and whose sins are covered up and completely buried." I felt a new beginning on the rise, unlike anything that I can even describe, but my healing process was not yet over.

It took months of digging into the depths of my soul to pull out the darkness. Getting rid of all the past years of dirty

168

secrets was like excavating giant piles of unwanted rubble, and as I uncovered my ugly realities, I felt tempted to give up many times. The constant upheaval of facing my pain to heal took more emotional energy than I felt I could endure. In the end, it was God that gave me the will to never give up, no matter what trials I was facing. With the comfort of God by my side, I suddenly found an immeasurable amount of courage within myself. One step at a time, I cleaned up every area of the unwanted mess living inside of me. The strength and stability that I gained from God's Word did not happen overnight but was a process. Unfortunately, I learned my lesson the hard way, but I finally sought-after God for the life that I was searching for all along.

The months passed by as I spent time diligently seeking God's next steps for my life. One small step at a time in this process led the way. After all that I uncovered within me, I learned that the remains of my marital state were the result of my own dissatisfaction. It took an enormous amount of courage to be able to finally come to terms with the disasters I caused both of us. I realized that my secret life of betrayal held me down like a ball and chain, and revealing the truth was the only way to freedom just as it says in John 16:13, "When the Spirit of truth comes, he will guide you into all truth." It also says in John 8:32, "The truth will set you free." I knew I could never truly move on with my life, and into my true calling, unless I was freed from the strongholds within me. I could have never written this book without facing the truth about taking the wrong direction in my life and destroying my family. With the newfound direction God had given me, I continued to gain more courage and face my problems. I accepted the responsibility for my life by doing whatever God had assigned me to do. I was to continue to allow God to make changes inside of my heart. My newfound journey was about my heart being made right with God. Then and only then would everything else in my life fall into place. This was not about me pointing my fingers at Mike anymore for what I thought he didn't do right in the past. It was my own bad attitude that led me to make even worse choices and became that wayward woman who was on the run for a long time.

The foundation of my relationship with God was in discovering the startling truth about myself, and the changes that were needed to pave the way to begin all over again. However, way off in my mind, I still had this inner conflict of not really coming to the full knowledge of truth. There was still this inner voice that kept whispering that I didn't choose the right husband, and yet, a big part of me was intent on being the kind of wife that I honestly wanted to be with Mike. It was truly a conflict inside of me that even I could not understand.

What I have written about my life in some of the following chapters will be hard for many to make sense of also. I know that as you continue to read about my journey, it may make your head spin, as it reveals how deceptive the enemy really is, and how Satan prowls around just looking to devour God's lost sheep. While on the outside my marriage was in a rebuilding process, on the inside I was still dealing with deception. I was not out of the woods yet, as I was still not seeing the whole truth that God desired for me to see.

Chapter 29

A Season of Coming Together

Six months had passed since my daughter's last visit home and Christmas was upon us. The expectancy of my daughter's arrival gave me a burst of energy. The areas of our lives that were in complete despair seemed to be finally on the mend. The opportunity for rekindling our relationship was finally awaiting us during the season that we loved the most.

Over the months, the memories of our tragedies seemed to fade away from our minds. My daughter and I were truly freed from the torment of our own bitterness. We were led by the pureness in our hearts and the eagerness to see each other again. In the months before Christmas, we dreamed of the upcoming weeks together. As the weeks were approaching, our plans for the season's celebration were led with great anticipation.

The thoughts of baking cookies led to the dreamy feeling of many holidays in the past. I shopped eagerly for all that was necessary to welcome her home. Not a detail was left undone to ensure this visit would be complete. The idea of gingerbread cookies baking in the oven filled my heart with sheer delight. Once again, our home would be a reminder of the good things we had done before as a family.

172

My mind briefly went back to the emptiness of our home during last year's Christmas. I had spent that holiday with the hopes that I would see her again. I kept my hopes up, as my health was at an all-time low. The stress had surely taken its final toll on me with the pressures of everything that went wrong in my life. I never wavered from the expectancy of my life to change. I don't know how I had the supernatural ability to soldier through the bleakness of everything that had fallen apart. God gave me a strength that I would not have had alone. As I looked back, I thanked God every single day for getting me through that especially horrible time in our lives.

I managed to get through last year's Christmas knowing that a new one would soon be on the horizon. I never questioned her reasons for not coming home that prior Christmas holiday. I knew that she would eventually return home again. Meanwhile, my priority was to continue onward, and allow God to mend our lives back together again in a healthy way. Just as the seasons changed from one to another, so did my life. Slowly but surely, I forged through it all. I was a warrior, relentless in my efforts to be a united family once again.

This Christmas season was very different from the last, we no longer held onto the former hurts from our past. I felt the pureness of our renewed hearts during this holiday visit. This season's excitement led our way into the three best weeks of my life. The opportunity to finally love each other again had an appreciation unlike ever before. Our hearts were warm and joyous in the season's arrival. This was truly the moment that I dreamed of since the day she left home fourteen months ago. This time, the tears were from the sheer laughter, nearly splitting our sides. The walls of isolation from one another were broken, and we were free to love each other once again. Resentful thoughts and feelings towards one another were no longer on anyone's agenda. The hurtful behaviors that previously hindered our connection had vanished and gave way for the love and laughter.

We baked cookies into all hours of the night and decorated each one of them for days on end. The decorating of the Christmas tree was euphoric in the reminiscence of every ornament. This took us back in time and reminded us of our special memories. We were able to relive the best of the previous years and cherished them.

We were as busy as elves preparing for the big family gathering on Christmas day. Finally having her home while preparing for the holidays filled my heart's desire. I had my daughter back again, and my best friend. We laughed so hard that the tears ran down our faces well into the midnight hour. The time we spent apart to have God heal each of our own wounds paid off. We were now blessed with our newfound relationship.

Having her home for the holidays was an absolute success. Finally, being with one another was long awaited. Her visit home exceeded anything that I could have imagined, and it was nothing short of God's best. Although I would have loved for her to stay home longer, I knew our time together

174

was quickly coming to an end. Her visit felt like it came to a crashing halt, and once again, so did my own life. I spent a month afterwards laying on the couch and missing her more than ever. I knew that she moved on with her own life, and yet somehow, I still didn't completely move on with mine. I was still hoping that she would find it in her heart to stay home and not go back to California ever again. The distance between us tore my dreams apart once again. I never imagined that we would end up over three thousand miles away from one another. Realizing the finality of her decision to live across the country hit me hard. I was filled with sadness, my dream was for her to stay home, but it was her dream to live in California.

Chapter 30

Daydreamer

As a little girl, the desire to be a princess always led me to the imaginary places inside my heart. Playing the role of a princess included everything that I desired. I dressed up in the frilliest of costumes that included my mother's old jewelry, dresses, makeup, and high heels. As my imagination wandered into the glorious passions of my heart, I felt awakened from the inside out. I was of course preparing myself for the prince that would one day find me to be his true love.

As I awaited the day of my prince's arrival, I dreamed that he would carry me away into an everlasting life of love. I was free as a bird to feel this dream flourish from within my soul. I didn't ever want to have the cynical mind of a woman who gave up on her dreams. However, shortly after my wedding day, I began realizing that my fairytale had not yet come true. I was already beginning to question if I had not married the man of my dreams. I began to think that my dream was not a realistic possibility, but rather only a fairytale.

Along this journey, I had read many articles from women explaining how their romantic daydreams never became a reality. So, they gave up on them. As I read through these articles, the deep expression of despair from within their hardened hearts moved me. I could relate to their disappointment and anguish, knowing the sad existence of giving up on one's true desires. I knew their lives would only become bitter with discontentment without any faith in their vision of a fulfilling marriage. It says in Proverbs 29:18 "Where there is no vision the people perish" and so does a marriage when we lose hope.

In the beginning of my faith filled journey, I realized how I had given up on the dreams that were still lingering in my heart. Without having the courage to fulfill my own dream of being in love, I knew my journey would never be complete, and neither would I. By studying scripture, God taught me that faith never gives up on a God-given dream. I realized that I had to have faith in all that God had placed inside of me. I was not only doing this for myself, but also to give hope to other women to follow their dream to be in love too.

It says in Psalms 37:4 "Delight yourself in the Lord and He will give you the desires and secret petitions of your heart." When I truly began embracing this scripture, the words became most meaningful in my life. This scripture spoke to me like no other, and I began to pursue it's meaning with all my heart. It has allowed me to take the time to reflect on the deepest parts of my soul. I realized that if I continued to drown out my dreams that I would have never quenched my heart's desires.

During this time, my prayers began revealing a part of my heart that was closed from the wounds in my past. The pain of my first true heartbreak at fifteen years old was suddenly brought back into my mind. God purposely brought me back to this painful moment to reveal that I never resolved this hurt. It was not about the boy hurting me; it was about my REACTION to the breakup that hurt me. God showed me this terrible moment of pain as if it were happening all over again. The pain revealed the fatal decision that I had made in the moment of feeling rejected. I made a vow to myself that I would never fall deeply in love again. I would suffer the detrimental consequences of this decision later in life.

Reliving that foolish decision revealed to me the true condition of my heart. I had eliminated the possibility of ever truly falling in love again. With my guard up, having the dream of true love was impossible. This was the heavy armor that I put around my heart, so that no one could ever hurt me again.

I was astonished that I had internalized my pain so deeply and was completely unaware of its destruction. I unknowingly carried this in my heart for over thirty years of my life. Until my deep moments of prayer, I did not remember this painful decision to close the windows to my heart. I had never searched my heart deep enough to remind me of this hurtful decision from my past. Suddenly, I knew it was all a part of God's plan to heal the brokenness inside of me.

This led me to ask God to open the hurting places inside of me that were guarded. I knew these were places deep within me that I never allowed anyone to reach. I felt an inner vacancy as my heart yearned for the kind of love that I had long waited for. It was as if the little girl inside of me kept screaming out from the fairytale of dreams to finally free my broken heart to be able to love again.

Sadly, I realized that I had become the kind of cynical woman who gave up on her dream to genuinely love others. Within my own defense system, I denied myself of the God-given ability to love someone so deeply to have this dream come true. Eventually, my guarded heart became the source of my shame and pain in my marriage. Sadly, I realized I was never wholeheartedly in my marriage to begin with. My spiritual awakening turned into the calling of my true heart's desires. Burying this dream would have meant that I could not write about what I have been shamefully hiding for over two decades.

Looking back for a moment, by the age of eight years old I had fantasies of the kind of man that I liked and pretended I'd marry one day. Recently, I began reflecting to my childhood daydreams. My mind began replaying the images of what this man looked like. I recalled T.V. shows and movies with the kind of men that captured my heart. They were always the type of men that were tough guys and raced hot rods. My earliest recollection of this type of man was in a T.V. show called Starsky and Hutch. After watching these episodes, I pretended to be the wife of Starsky in my childhood daydreams.

By the time that I was eleven years old I fell in love with a popular movie named Grease, with John Travolta and Olivia Newton John. I fell madly in love with not only the movie, but the role of John Travolta. His image was a tough guy that built race cars and dragged raced them for money. Every time I watched this movie, somewhere deep inside of me was the image of the man of my dreams. Only a few years later, I wound up singing the song "I honestly love you" by Olivia Newton John in a talent show to my heartthrob teenage boyfriend who was the same one who eventually broke my heart.

Throughout my life, I had an imaginary man of my dreams. It seemed as if the image was already etched into the blueprint of my mind. Some days, I couldn't shake this image in my mind, no matter how hard I tried. I was always stuck inside of a daydream and was not able to see it through. Over the course of my marriage there was always this unsatisfied feeling for the man of my dreams, and it was growing with a fury, as my marriage was slowly dwindling away.

Chapter 31

Discontented Wife

I knew the day I met Mike that he had integrity in his character and was the kind of man that I envisioned for marriage. After our very first conversation together, I knew deep down that he would be the man that I would eventually marry. While deciding to spend the rest of my life with him was most definitely a conscious decision at the time, I was not wholehearted about any decision I made at that state of my maturity. Somehow, even back then, I knew my heart could not be trusted. It says in Jeremiah 17:9, "The heart is deceitful above all things and beyond cure who can understand it?" My soul was wounded and filled with pain from my teenage years, and I was unable to give myself freely to Mike.

Many years later, he found that I was completely distanced from loving him. In sheer desperation of not knowing what love really was, I clung onto my own ideas of marriage. Despite his efforts of changing himself to meet my constantly ever-changing needs, he only came up against my dissatisfaction towards him. His attempt at trying to make me happy, in as many ways that he could, including buying me new cars, clothes, and jewelry, nearly emptied our bank accounts. This steep price of loving me was all a part of what I thought the ideal marriage was supposed to be. My worldly experiences had taught me that love was all about what a man could do to love me with materialism ... but buying me the expensive things I admired only made matters worse.

I anticipated marriage since childhood, but what I didn't know was that I was anxiously seeking to fulfill the emptiness inside of me, rather than truly loving the husband of my dreams. Instead of looking to God, I looked to Mike to fulfill my deepest thirst for love, and without realizing the truth, I wasn't even remotely prepared to receive or give love. Unknowingly, my plans were essentially to spend the rest of my life relying on him for what only God could fill inside of me. When I wanted to feel worthy, I looked to my husband. When I wanted to feel loved unconditionally, I sought it from my husband. When I wanted to feel comforted, cherished, validated, or encouraged, I relied entirely on my husband. Inevitably, my husband let me down, and in those moments that he could not fulfill my needs completely, I felt unworthy and unloved. I understand now that this unattainable quest was a recipe for disaster. My marriage expectations that were formed in my childhood were hidden in the deep places of my heart ... and my notions of life and marriage had devastating effects. The more that I looked to Mike for the kind of love that only God could give, the emptier I became. I was unaware of the devastating effects my unmet expectations had on both me and him. I wanted to ignore this voice inside of me that was calling me to take responsibility for placing such unreasonable expectations on him to be everything for me.

I set Mike up for failure when I expected him to fulfill me completely, and whenever I tried to make him fit that role, it only hurt him. I unintentionally made him an idol above God believing he could fulfill me more than God could. My own frustration escalated and led to many volatile arguments with him. I never hesitated to blame him about my feelings of not having enough, or to blame him for never being enough to meet my needs. My discontentment grew, and my sense of entitlement only made me more of a demanding wife who thought, "I deserve better". My unmet expectations lit a raging fire within me. During my demands, I exhausted Mike, but continued to believe that I always deserved the best of everything. The tension created in our marriage eventually spread to our children. My lack of a proper perspective negatively affected everyone in our home.

As I reflected over my behavior during this time, I realized how it sent my daughter into a complete state of anxiousness. This made me feel like a failure as a mother. God opened my eyes to the destruction of my discontentment. God needed to transform my thinking once again, and the only way He could do that was if I humbled myself and let go of my unreasonable expectations. This process didn't happen overnight, but it continued to mature me a little bit every day. I began to find satisfaction in my faith and gratitude for the things Mike provided over the years. God showed me the value of being a wife of faith, a wife who trusts in Him, and who is confident in her own identity of worthiness and purpose. I believed that as I chose to walk in the Spirit, love would continually pour out of me, and bless my marriage and family. I knew that I could have a thriving marriage, but it would require many steps of faith to finally come to that place of contentment.

Chapter 32

Too Busy Being in Love

As early as my teenage years, I searched from one relationship to another to find true love. I would call it chain dating. There was not a moment in time that lapsed from one relationship to another. From the time that I was eleven years old, I was never alone without a boyfriend in my life. When I looked back, I wondered where my heart was in this never-ending mix of boys. I was trying to find me inside of these relationships ... but the love that was missing inside of me would never be found in them.

As I was growing up, finding my identity was never emphasized. The only emphasis seemed to be that one day I was expected to get married and have children. Later in life, my attempt at finding my sense of worth and identity became virtually impossible to do because of the mountain of insecurities I had built up over many years. It became apparent to me that the generation of women before me were in the same boat as I was, and they couldn't teach me what they didn't know. So, I learned from their flawed perspectives on the meaning and purpose for my own life. Unfortunately, I relied solely upon the boys, and eventually men, in my life for my identity.

As each year passed, the chances of finding my true self dwindled even further. It wasn't that I didn't ever try to find my identity; it was simply that I was unaware of who God was, and what He wanted me to do with my life. I made many attempts searching for what I thought I desired without God, only to find out later that I somehow felt trapped in a meaninglessness life. My frustration was always this feeling that there was something more I was meant to do. In trying to find myself, I surrendered my own identity to my relationships. I also relied on people's opinions about what I should do with my life, based on how they saw me through their own eyes. The answer that eluded me was waiting with God, but my reliance on others was still too strong to allow me to search beyond human perception, will, and emotion.

With each rebound from one boyfriend to the next, I was led further away from discovering my identity. Consequently, the overwhelming need to be in these never-ending relationships sustained the passions that I never allowed myself to find personally. These false passions kept me safe from the hard fall of my own neglect to find my identity. I always felt as if I was just a giant nobody, looking for someone else to cover for me. With each passing relationship, I lost another piece of my soul.

I was too busy being "in love" to allow God's love to fill me with identity and purpose. Romance falsely kept me in a safe place from having to face the shame of not knowing who I really was. My relationships became the addiction that tried to satisfy the vacancy I felt inside. They were a sad attempt at hiding behind the fact that I was not living the life that was meant for me. I buried any glimmer of hope of being anyone special. Every step that I took in romantic relationships was a trade-off for the life that God really wanted for me. My life fell completely short of the mark. How disappointing things had become without my own personal journey with God.

After saying "I DO" to my husband over twenty years before, I found myself amongst the broken ruins of my marriage. This mess wasn't because of what Mike didn't do for me. It was because I never recognized what I should do to find myself. I not only fell short in my own life, but I fell short of being all that I should have been for my family. Once and for all, I realized that I needed to be complete in the woman I was meant to be, rather than too busy "being in love" to know who I was in Christ.

Chapter 33

The Marital Struggle

Over the course of my marriage, my sense of uneasiness only escalated. My mind seemed to be in a never-ending controversy over the matters of my heart. This war within me eventually fought its way to the final round. I spent decades thinking about the possibilities for my future. My thoughts never led me to a solution or any sense of peace because I was too caught up in the vicious cycle of my unhappiness. Listening to my mind playing out hopeless scenarios about my life and marriage sounded like a broken record.

As I continued along on my own path of destructive thoughts, I only distanced myself from the life that I desired having. My doubts and disbelief of who I was or wasn't kept me chained inside an unfulfilled marriage, and it only left me in need of something more profound. A deeper feeling of love was still something my heart was yearning to have, and yet I couldn't seem to find it, no matter how far I would run. My emotional struggles were becoming more apparent as the years went on.

Over time, this heartless feeling fell completely short of the life that I dreamed of having. There was a restlessness from within that always kept me with one foot out the door.

Although I tried desperately to suppress my dissatisfied thoughts and feelings, they eventually came up and out of my mouth like a volcanic eruption. Over the years, my heart continued to fall to pieces, and so did our marriage. Eventually we were left amongst the broken pieces together. I spent years unable to find the solutions and was frightened by the constant thoughts of where my life was headed.

It was nearly two decades after we married that I found the courage to discuss with him the unspoken words of how I thought I was not in love with him. After breaking this news to him our hearts felt as if they had completely broken. We were tormented by the reality of the terrible state in which we wound up. We had no idea which way to turn next, and after everything we had been through, I was still alluding to the idea of divorce and breaking his heart all over again.

We continued to strive within our own efforts to see if we could somehow find love in our marriage. In the exhausting effort to do so, we had both finally come to the end of our rope. We were brought to our knees in need of the power of prayer and wisdom. We placed our trust in God, knowing He would show us exactly what to do next. Finally, our faith and trust in God anchored both of us to a sense of inner peace and lifted the heavy burden of all our troubles. It was a miraculous experience, and there are really no words to describe how God seemed to ease our hearts and minds once both of us surrendered our marital problems to Him.

We went on with our everyday lives, trusting in God and allowing Him to lead our way. The level of unshakable faith that we needed was the biggest challenge of all. Our lives had to go on together unless we thought that God directed us to do differently. No matter what my heart was feeling in this marriage, I wanted to be sure that God would show both of us the truth. It says in Matthew 10:26, "Nothing is ever concealed that would not be revealed." I knew we both needed time with God to have the truth come to light.

Regardless of our circumstances, we needed to see things through and continue in the marriage. Even though our lives together were still falling apart, we knew our marriage was the covenant that we made before God. As it says in Matthew 19:6, "So they are no longer two, but one flesh. Therefore, what God had joined, let no man separate" and I took these words to heart, even though at times, I still wanted to run away from home.

As I reflected over the years before we were married, my heart kept telling me that I was not ready for the commitment of marriage yet. I distinctly remember turning a deaf ear to this voice inside of me and warning me not to marry, until I was ready. It was only after being awakened to the utter destruction in our marriage that I realized I wasn't ready for any relationship, until I built one with God.

I spent the years wondering why I should stay in the constant feelings of a failed marriage, but as Mike and I faced our problems together, we finally began praying together, and asking God for the wisdom to solve our marital problems. We began studying the verses on marriage together and learned that God said, "He hates divorce".

I thought a lot about what God said about divorce, but as I thought even further about our circumstances, I still made excuses to somehow justify getting a divorce, and I even tried twisting the scriptures to suit my selfish desire to do so. I thought there must have been an exception for divorce. After all, I thought that God wanted me to be happy! I also knew that staying together in misery was not the solution to our problems. I honestly believed the two of us were completely incompatible, and there didn't seem to be a chance for us to ever live in harmony. I felt that we did not seem to have any chance of a happy life together. The thought of going on as we had in the past had scared me more than I could have ever put into words. I did not want to settle for less than what my heart desired anymore.

I figured that God did not want me to sacrifice myself for the sake of this miserable marriage. I believed that God was the God of hearts, and He didn't want me to just co-exist in a bad marriage, but rather to discover what love really was in a good one. I would've only been fooling myself if I believed that I could continue to live in our marriage the way it was because it didn't suit either of our needs, but every time that I dug deeper into God's Word, I found nothing that would excuse me from my marriage.

Regardless of our marital circumstances, I knew that God was leading me to live according to biblical truth. This helped me realize that it would be the beginning of healing for myself and our marriage. Slowly but surely, I began to discover my biblical roles as a wife. I realized the only way to save my soul, and our marriage, would be to do things God's way first and foremost.

Chapter 34

Virtuous Woman

I was reluctant, but obedient, to learn about the virtuous woman (The Wife of Noble Character) as described in Proverbs 31:10-31, and this was my next destination. The virtuous woman respected her husband by bringing him goodness all the days of her life. She was a woman whose primary role was to work at home taking care of her family. She made clothes for them, fed them, and watched over the affairs in her household. She was a woman who saw that her family's money needed to be used wisely. She extended her arms to the poor and hands to the needy. She spoke with wisdom, and faithful instruction was on her tongue. Her children call her blessed and her husband praised her. She was to be honored for all that she had done, and her works brought her praise from the city gates.

When I read this biblical chapter, I realized that I had only three of the virtues described in the woman I was to become. So, I looked at the bright side of things, knowing that I had already accomplished at least some parts of this role. I thought to myself, "How difficult could the rest of this possibly be for me." As I went further into my studies however, I learned there was even more to this virtuous woman than I originally thought.

It says in Ephesians 5:22, "Wives submit to your husbands as you do to the Lord." I thought Proverbs 31 was a challenge, but this verse seemed even more so. After a while, I settled down and thought maybe I only had to submit to what we agreed upon as husband and wife. As I read even further, it said in Ephesians 5:24, "Wives submit to your husbands in everything." The word "EVERYTHING" stood out in my mind, as I painfully envisioned all that this could mean for me.

I thought, "How could this be true?" I searched the scriptures to see if I could find it in a different context. Maybe I would find it in another verse teaching us to submit to our husbands only on birthdays, anniversaries, and Valentine's Day. Well, I diligently searched the Bible's scriptures and came across 1 Peter 3:5, "For this is the way of the holy women of the past who put their hope in God used to adorn themselves and they submitted themselves to their own husbands." As well in Colossians 3:18 "Wives submit yourselves to your husbands, as fitting in the Lord." It went on and on!

I knew there was simply no way out of this because it was plainly written multiple times throughout the bible and there was no possible way to misinterpret its meaning. The next scripture I came across finalized it for me, as it was clearly written out in Ephesians 5:23, "The husband is the head of the wife as Christ is the head of the church." Then I thought to myself, "This was a completely different era, and it was no longer current in its use." Well, that thought didn't last too long because as I studied further, I found a scripture in

Hebrews 13:8. It reads, "Jesus Christ is the same yesterday and today and forever." This meant to me that biblical use is ALWAYS current and applicable to our lives today. Then, I finally read in Hebrews 13:4, "Marriage should be honored." The revelation of this scripture for me was to honor all of what the previous scriptures had stated. It pointed out to me everything I didn't honor and wound-up destroying.

I thought however, "What was God thinking when He made this to-do list for me?" After a while I did manage to simmer down and realized that God purposely saved this challenging part of my journey for last. I was exhausted just thinking about becoming this virtuous woman, and as my eyes glazed over, I looked back over Mike's past birthdays, remembering how submitting to him just for a day was like a triathlon for me. As this memory from the past flashed before me, I felt my lazy days and lack of honor suddenly drifting away. The woman that I needed to become was indeed going to be a very productive woman on a mission, and I was going to be a woman who submitted to (and honored) my husband with complete trust in God for His ultimate plan of marriage. I had to humble myself to submit to God's ultimate plan for a marriage. So, I took a deep breath, and moved forward to finally become the virtuous woman I was created to be.

Chapter 35

Heart Matters

It seemed nearly impossible to find enough time to do things with my own life anymore. There was simply no room for anything, besides being the virtuous wife as depicted in Proverbs 31 and Titus 2. Evidently, I didn't own my life anymore. It was obvious that God did not want me to do anything other than making Mike a priority, because as the Bible says, "We were no longer two but one." As his suitable helper, I needed to submit and align myself to him. As it says in Genesis 2:18 "Now the Lord God said it is not good that the man should be alone. I will make him a help meet (suitable, adapted, and complimentary) for him." Ever since this journey began, I surrendered one area of my life at a time to be God's servant and adhering to His precepts were the only way I'd ever know who I truly was as a woman of God.

However, I also needed to fulfill the calling to complete my book, and this meant choosing my time wisely when Mike was working. So, reprioritizing my days in this order was a great lesson. As the months passed, I learned that the only way I could ever be successful at fulfilling God's will was to remain focused on my primary role as a submissive wife, and everything else in my life would follow.

Becoming intimate in a marriage on an emotional, spiritual, and physical realm was the plan. I began believing that being separated from one another and having entirely different agendas did not seem to fit God's plan for us as plainly written in Genesis 2:24, "Therefore a man shall leave his mother, and shall cleave to his wife." Both of us having our days filled with a bunch of diverse interests seemed to me as a life of coexisting in a contractual type of marriage. It seemed we were always at a distance and living worlds apart.

Up until now, our lives were separated by our own independent selfish desires, but as we both continued our personal journey seeking God, I began seeing glimpses of us becoming more intertwined with one another. We were finally seeing well beyond ourselves and began supporting each other's desires to accomplish some of our own personal dreams, presently being my book and his business. I still however, wanted our lives to be on an even deeper level of commitment with something more in common together every day. This common goal, whatever it was, was still missing between us, and we still weren't sure of exactly what God's future for us were. Maybe there wasn't a common goal ... other than just two people who were willing to do whatever God asked us to do by unselfishly seeking the best interests of one another. I learned much later; this was the most important goal.

I was trying so hard to give our marriage my best shot, but I began noticing that I couldn't seem to fulfill my role of submission properly when self-gratification was my only goal. I was awakened to the fact that although I was trying to submit to my husband, for some reason I was failing horribly. I realized that I was not trusting God fully in this department. I prayed over this and realized that God was the One who said, "Mike was the leader and I was to respond to him as his helper." Was it as simple as surrendering myself entirely to my husband and nothing more? I was submitting to the things that I thought I should, but still wasn't following my husband's lead. I was whining and complaining in my heart, wondering how in the world I could even find fulfillment in this role as a wife! I thought there was a far better reason for my life than being someone's servant when suddenly I heard in my mind, "Really?" I had no clue about sacrificial love. No clue whatsoever! It was always about me.

I knew deep down that I needed to live my life ultimately for the Lord, and to do that by what He was calling me to do as a wife and a mother. Certainly, being a wife was a part of my calling, and yet my heart could not deny that I still had personal desires from as far back as I could remember. Was God asking me to sacrifice my own desires for the sake of HIM? I came to believe that the answer was "yes"- He was. It seemed that I could not choose to live a double life anymore, and if my personal interests were selfishly conflicting with my marriage, I was to sacrifice, and let them go! God wanted me to quit bouncing all over the place and fulfill His will, not my own.

I was finally in this marriage to give it everything that I had by honoring God first. If God asked me to hang upside down from a flimsy tree branch by my toenails, even after a fresh pedicure, there's no question that I would have done so by this point. Any doubts that I had about honorably submitting to Mike were not so simply resolved however, even though I was trusting in the Lord's overall plans for my life, as much faith was needed to sacrifice and surrender my will to His.

For now, I knew my personal mission was to complete my book. All I knew for sure was that my personal calling was to write about my journey and use it as a resource of wisdom that would one day serve many other women who were in the same boat as me. This was my God-given mission, but I knew my own recovery and wholeness was not yet fully attained. At times, I felt quite challenged with this recovery, and wondered if I would ever be whole, but my faith knew that God would finish the work that He started in me.

Chapter 36

The Sacrifice

I never knew who I truly was as a wife from the very beginning, and I struggled immensely during my journey with doubting thoughts about submitting to Mike unequivocally on his final decisions. I feared that in the role of being a submissive wife, I'd have to give up my own personal ideas and interests for the sake of his preferences. I feared that I would lose myself in him and become miserably unsatisfied with my own life all over again.

I asked myself if I could really sacrifice the idea of becoming some type of independent woman who pursued her own ideas and followed her own heart, regardless of how it would negatively affect my family. Could I go on and be everything for Mike, as if it was all about him? I thought there would be absolutely nothing left of me, but God wasn't asking me to be everything for Mike at all. My perspective was wrong. I needed to be the type of unselfish woman who had more concern for her family's well-being than only for herself. I also wondered though if I could I ever consider my family above myself once and for all when it came to important decisions in my life?

Even though these uncertain thoughts that I faced were overwhelming, my prayer life kept setting me straight. I knew that God was most certain in His plan for my life, and during it all, I had come to realize that being a submissive wife wasn't all for the sake of Mike. I was to pick up the cross for the sake of my new discovery called sacrificial love, knowing in my heart that it reflected Jesus and His covenant of dying for the sake of us. According to scripture, I would never lose myself on this new path laid out before me because it says quite clearly "Whoever wants to save their life will lose it, but whoever loses their life for me will find it," (Matthew 16:25).

I was just beginning to see a clear picture of what the act of love really looked like, and in the past, I had been completely off base. One of the reasons that Mike and were not in sync with one another, was simply because I was not submitting honorably to him and following God's order. There were so many things out of order that needed to be addressed. The first of them all was overcoming the chaos living inside of me. I needed to make peace with myself first and foremost. It was like a tug of war to finally surrender my flesh and allow the Holy Spirit to renew my soul. All along it was my own selfish disguise that led me to believe I deserved whatever I wanted just to be happy, but my life had only fallen into a million pieces.

Without even knowing, I had become lost and confused by the world's feministic agenda and their cultural ideas for women. As I was fighting desperately to find myself, and where I fit in as a wife amongst this confusion, I realized that I was far from the image of Christ as His bride. The world's idea of marriage had depicted a completely different image of the roles as husband and wife, and there I was, left with only a poor example of what marriage was really supposed to be.

I found myself just going through the motions of being this submissive wife, and yet, neither of us had any satisfaction from my halfhearted efforts. I was still searching and struggling to become the image of this wife that both my husband and I longed for, but the role I was trying to fulfill as a wife left out a very important element which was to have passion for him. All my sacrificing looked more like the role of a maid or a personal assistant, not a wife. The goal of becoming his suitable helper was looking more and more like a soldier answering to the call of duty. My marriage became merely a display of a sacrificial ceremony with nothing more than striving in my own efforts to the point of exhaustion ... along with my burnt offerings for dinner. It seemed the more I tried to become what I thought God wanted, the more trouble I wound up causing for both of us. I was noticeably awkward trying to fulfill this role as a submissive wife in the act of my own flesh. Without a true passion for him, there was absolutely nothing redeeming about my efforts.

Mike wasn't falling for my act. He would have much preferred that I forgot about my fake dutiful services, and instead wrap my arms around him as the love of my life, but

I just wasn't there yet. It was a sheer struggle to let go of trying to be the wife that I thought I should've always been and trust God to do the work in me instead. It became obvious to me that I was still not letting go of "self" in order to rebuild my marriage and family. I was still not trusting, not fully trusting, or believing this is what God wanted for my life. Within my struggles, I realized that I was never fully committed to the vows I had made to my him long ago. I was becoming a different woman now through the grace of God, and I was finally being prepared, no matter how hard it was going to be, to begin to love my him with all my heart.

I could finally see that many of my problems were caused by simply not trusting in God's plans for my life. I no longer wanted to protect myself from the fear of losing "self" in building my relationship with God. I went full tilt with an unshakable faith into a spiritual realm that I didn't even know existed. I finally began to let go. I quit striving within my own efforts to try to control everything, know everything, and trying to outwit God. Thankfully, I discovered that God was not calling me to become an imposter, and pretend to be in love anymore, as I mistakenly thought He was. I knew by now that I could not force anything or try to change things about myself. My life was going to be God's way if I wanted things to change at all.

My heart needed to transform, and growth was needed to occur before any type of honorable reverence for Mike could happen. It took a ton of meditation on God's Word to begin to transform my heart and mind. It was revealed to me in

Romans 5:5 that the very type of love that I needed is indeed poured out within our hearts through the Holy Spirit. Although I had not yet evolved into a love that was complete, I believed my heart was softening and beginning to change forever. I believed it was finally the opening that would bring both my husband and I closer together than ever before.

It took several years before God had made a noticeable overhaul in my heart and mind. With one step at a time, I adapted to my husband as a submissive wife, and his desire to be the head of our family. Low and behold, we began dreaming of a future together. In my ever-reverent worship for God, a genuine love and passion for him was developing. In the struggle of finally giving all of myself, I found an even deeper love for him, and we were finally beginning to build a wonderful life together.

It turned out that sacrificing my life for the sake of doing what was right for my family was personally more gratifying and fulfilling than anything ever was before. There was no denying that giving more of myself unselfishly was the very thing that fulfilled my heart.

Chapter 37

Ready to Love Again

A big part of my resentment towards Mike was since he loved me just the way I was, while I didn't. I thought to myself many times, "How could he possibly love me?" My anger towards him was just anger at myself. I didn't want to be loved as this broken-hearted woman who was not being the best she could be. I felt like a failure on the inside and wanted no part of him loving me in a broken state. I questioned myself many times as to why he wanted to love a broken woman in the first place. What kind of unresolved inner need did he have that my brokenness wound up on his lap? Probably, any professional counselor could have a field day with this one, because two broken halves do not make a whole marriage. Therefore, the problems we were having couldn't have just been because of me. There are two sides to every dysfunctional marriage. In this case, it was two people living together, but broken, and for some reason, many times Mike unintentionally played the role of my Savior.

Throughout the years, I pushed him further away from what little love there was in my heart. While I was in this broken state, I was unable to truly love anyone, including myself. My heart felt like a lump of coal as the years went on. Finally, I had no other choice than to become willing to open my heart again, no matter what the circumstances were in our marriage. My trust to remain faithful to this marriage was because of my overall trust in God's ultimate plan. I did not use sense and reason anymore to believe that I could ever get myself out of this mess alone. I knew that God would set everything right through my faith in Him. My faith in God, and my actions that followed, were changing everything in ways that I never imagined were possible.

As I kept peeling more layers back, I asked God, "How could I grow to love Mike more deeply?" I knew there were still more places inside of my heart that were undiscovered, and I wanted to have a love between us that I would be more capable of sharing. This question began to change me in ways beyond anything I dreamed were possible. I kept opening my heart for God's love to continually work on renewing me inside and out. Living breath to breath with God and discovering His love had awakened the empty and desolate places within me. My desire to give and receive love grew more ... and I was finally beginning to have this sense of freedom that I never had before. It was a true freedom that kept me from trying to run away and hide in a life of lies.

At first, I realized I was hesitant to open my heart to love Mike too deeply. I thought many times to myself, "What if I dive in too deep and become hurt like so many times before?' But as I furthered my relationship with God, my trust in Him replaced any fear or hesitation. I was no longer protecting my heart from being hurt. I finally had the greatest Savoir on earth! With my identity growing evermore in Christ, I was filled with a love. It was different, not like the kind of "love" based on an emotional feeling, but rather was rooted in the deep and everlasting love of God. My relationships were not because of what others could do for me, but was about my choice to love others, and treat them more significantly. This newfound love was based on knowing that as a child of God, I was finally being filled with His love first (1 John 4:19).

God's love as described in 1 Corinthians 13:4-8, is enduring, patient, kind, never envious nor boastful, or conceited. It is not rude or insisting on its own way. This love is not self-seeking, resentful, and especially never pays attention to when evil is done to it. This kind of love was a new revelation to me, and I was ready to believe the best of my husband. This was the type of love that allowed us to begin growing in harmony together.

Over these healing years, I had to take care of myself spiritually, physically, and emotionally. I had to clear away any pain from my past by facing every ounce of it. Little by little, I was emerging out of denial by facing my past, as God gave me the true desires of my heart in every area of my life. It was becoming apparent to me that this included my love life with Mike, and God began revealing my sexual desires for him as well. Honestly, I never ventured into this journey believing that God was going to heal me sexually. I didn't even realize that I was sexually bound up from the painful things I had internalized from my past.

My healing was about my change of perspective and knowing that hurting people will only hurt other people. The way others had treated me in the past (or in the future) would not be a gage as to whether I was worthy of love or not. I no longer carried these unresolved issues of love into any of my relationships. All the pain of rejection was gone. I would no longer base my feelings or reactions off other people's actions towards me, and therefore I was no longer a victim of my own despair. As a woman of God, I was no longer a reflection of anyone else. How I felt about myself was no longer a reflection of how I was treated in the past or in the future. I would live by my own standards and principles according to God. I would be the kind of woman who would depend solely on God to define myself, knowing that God is love.

After the affairs were over, I blocked the idea of ever being sexual again. The immense effort it took to have pleasure was not fun. I would sweat and shake uncontrollably, trying so hard to come to this place of ecstasy, but not enjoying myself. Mike looked like he just came out of the ring from an exhausting fight just from trying to please me. The poor guy. I began praying to God about this problem. Neither one of us wanted sex to become a relentless effort that was completely unsatisfying for both of us.

I reflected and began asking God why it was so difficult to achieve sexual pleasure in the later years of my marriage. As I continued to pray about this, God placed in my heart that it was because of the icy-cold state of my bitter soul. I knew that I didn't feel right inside, and I knew that in the troubled years of our marriage, my negative thoughts about myself (and my husband) had led me into this "Frigid Zone". This was only made worse because of my affairs; whose darkness left my womanhood and soul in a state of major shut-down.

As the months progressed, I was led to pray for healing from every single wound which stemmed from my impurity. I began noticing that sex no longer required me to be an endurance athlete. I never mentioned that I felt this healing change inside of me to Mike, but he was noticing the difference. I think we both knew that my womanhood was recovering, and I was ready to love again, but once again I would sabotage our progress. Selfishness was once again pulling on me from my distorted childhood images of "being in love."

As relationship challenges and differences of opinions rose between Mike and I, our marriage once again seemed to not fit what I was expecting or looking for. My selfishness pulled me backwards when we were faced with these new challenges between us. During these times, I heard an ever so faint voice in the back of my mind whispering, "this isn't going to work out." Unfortunately, this led to the beginning of more trouble for me and our marriage.

That same voice whispering lies to me suggested that there must be someone else who knew how to love me better. I was mistakenly idealizing a perfect relationship in which I didn't have to work so hard. Being in love with my "Mr.

Perfect" should be easy I thought, and I began to derail my marriage once again by searching for someone who "seemed a better fit" than my husband apparently was. I needed to find "The one and only made for me ... my secret soulmate." "Where is he, I thought to myself?" The Devil was shrewd and never gave up in whispering the lie that Mike was not "The One" and this is where everything took another unimaginable turn for the worse.

Chapter 38

My Imaginary Man

I had decided that it was finally time for me to visit California. There was absolutely no denying that as I looked at all that God had done in my life, I realized He had orchestrated the entire course of events since my daughter left home. My answered prayer for a Christian mentor was the tie that directly connected my daughter in California and myself in New York. Although her life was still separated from mine, we were both on a rapid pace of growth. Although there were miles between us, we were somehow similarly preparing for greater things to come.

I realized the importance of my prayers for my daughter that I said every day. They would never be underestimated, or overlooked, throughout the rest of my life. If it were not for these faith-filled prayers, I would not want to imagine where my daughter would have wound up, or if she would still be alive today. My prayers intercepted her plans to travel alone and live in unsafe places. The harsh reality of the city streets in Hollywood were swarming with human traffickers. She was just a naive, innocent eighteen-year-old girl with nothing more than one suitcase, and a knapsack on her back filled with a of lot money. She must have stuck out like a sore thumb, but the power of prayer kept a wall of protection around her, and the right people were miraculously sent to help save her life. It was only by the pure grace of God that my prayers were answered.

As I was preparing myself for my visit to California, I was reminded to reflect upon my life. The Holy Spirit brought me back with remembrance of all that He had revealed to me in the past. He brought me to the visions that I had still not yet been able to make sense of. I searched my heart for the vital parts of my life that I still did not understand. It would still be several years until I would come to understand the truth about myself that God was revealing to me.

As my life appeared to the outside world, one would think there would be no way I had visions that were plaguing me for decades. I knew however, as it says in Samuel 16:7, "Man looks on the outward appearance, but the Lord looks at the heart." God knew my heart, and he knew that these were the major areas in my life that needed to be uncovered.

For years, I suppressed the truth about my visions to avoid getting to the core of my problems. It was not that I wanted to go on pushing down anything inside of me, but I never had anyone to help me overcome what I had suffered with inside. During this part of my journey, I don't believe that I was even consciously aware that there was still a part of me living in doubt, or the doublemindedness I held about my marriage until I was confronted with the truth about it.

It was beyond my ability to comprehend the great big picture for my life, but living in the fear of the unknown, and suppressing the truth, were no longer something that I could tolerate. This caused me to finally realize a key point in my life that had been unresolved for years.

The confusing thoughts that had been stirring around in my mind for decades all began with my childhood image of the fantasy man of my dreams. As the years went on in my marriage, the fantasy of this image overtook my daily thoughts. It was my form of escapism from the troubles I was having in my marriage. I was already well into my marriage when something inside of me was whispering to me about the man of my dreams. I knew through the visions in my mind that the man I was married to still did not seem to be this perfect man that I was imagining. There were glimpses in the back of my mind of a blueprint for my "perfect husband", but I couldn't make out the face of this man. My visions revealed a side profile in a dark shadow of him. I had fantasized of this vague image for so long that it seemed as real as life itself.

Over the course of my marriage, I attempted to give up on the idea of this image. I took a new direction and blocked out the imaginary man because the thoughts only confused me, distanced myself from Mike, and caused me more pain. Years had passed by, and when my marital troubles seemed insurmountable, the images began to pop back into my mind.

One day, I was feeling empty and lonely, and I had a longing for the great reminders of this imaginary man again. The image appeared in my mind with a side profile of him once again. However, the desire of this image was stronger than ever before, and I began having an uneasy feeling that I had

213

married the wrong man. I made every attempt to find satisfaction with Mike anyway, but every effort left me hopeless. I just knew in my heart that the man I married didn't seem to be the imaginary man in my mind.

My secret image was etched deep down inside of my mind. I couldn't ever tell a living soul about my vision because I feared that anyone hearing about it would believe I had lost my mind ... and now that I think back, maybe I did. I relied on this image as my only hope to find the man of my dreams. This image became my numbing fantasy and comfort zone in my lowest and loneliest moments. My thoughts and delusions kept me searching and running to find a "soulmate."

In my confusion, I kept opening the doors to this delusional idea which seemed to comfort me. Eventually, the idea became a small voice which whispered with more clarity than ever before that someone was coming into my life. The voice said clearly, "You don't have to look for him, he will find you." When I heard this message, it was as if someone had whispered it directly into my ear. I was so attracted to this message that it became my personal destiny, which I fully accepted and believed to be true.

My quest for this person entering my life was fortified several months later when I heard the same thing again being whispered to me in my mind. I looked around me this time to see if anyone was coming towards me. Again, I heard the voice say, "You don't have to look for him, he will find you." I thought to myself, "This is the second time that I am certain

214

I heard this unusual message", and it thrilled me with mysterious expectation, just like the romance novels that I once read long ago.

My decision to visit my daughter in California was based on many of my needs and desires. A year before my daughter ran away, I knew that my life needed direction, and I had prayed about it. My prayer was answered after my daughter's disappearance with the promise of a Christian mentor to help me. This resulted from my new acquaintance with my husband's old friend John who lived not far from my daughter in Los Angeles. Only a few months earlier, after my daughter's runaway, I was shaken to the core with the reality of my life's troubles. This was the very moment I knew that my life needed to change!

After informing John about the bad news of my daughter's disappearance, I was hoping for a miracle, and that somehow, he would find her in Los Angeles. As I have mentioned earlier in the book, a few days later, I received a call from John's best friend Sammy, who was a Christian mentor. I knew from my conversations with John that Sammy had a ministry of some kind and helped people. When we spoke for the first time, he informed me that he had ministered to many runaway kids before. I suddenly began raising an eyebrow at what I like to call a lot of "God-incidences", or unexplainable coincidences. I knew there was no possible way that this story was coming together by chance. It was the work of God's hands over our lives. This Christian mentor that I prayed for came into my life just in the nick of time, and out of nowhere! At the time, I couldn't figure out if I did something wrong to have God's favor in my life, or right. The bottom line is that God is good even when the circumstances are not.

Within only a couple of weeks, Sammy became my personal Christian mentor. Sometime later, after I re-established contact with my daughter, I suggested that she contact Sammy, which she did, initially to accept his help in pursuing her dream of becoming a singer/songwriter, but along the way he became her personal Christian mentor, as well as his personal assistant Janeen, who was a singer/songwriter that helped her on the path of making music. It was no coincidence that Shannon had everything lined up perfectly for her. Sammy helped accelerate many of the positive changes within both of our lives. I often thought, "Where would we be today, if it weren't for all of this man's help." His life exemplified giving to those who were in need wherever and whenever possible. My daughter and I were blessed to have him help guide us to rebuild our lives.

I mentioned earlier that first time I saw Sammy on his ministry website page, I was completely captured by the sight of him. The very first picture that I saw of him was a profile picture of him and the look of love pouring out onto the multitudes of people. I can't explain it, but immediately I saw myself in his life. What I mean by this is that I identified with his life as the kind of life that I wanted as well. In other words, I saw myself (the real me) doing what he was doing throughout the pictures on his ministry website. This was a vision inside of me that accelerated my desire to attain the goal of ministry through sharing my story.

It wasn't until later however, that I realized his profile picture stood out in my mind for some other reason as well. I must have gone back to that picture of him at least fifty times, but the seemingly stark resemblance of his image to the imaginary dream man in my previous visions had not yet dawned on me. Until one day, out of nowhere it hit me! I thought there was a significant resemblance between my imaginary man and my mentor. I thought, can this be the man I have been searching for, or was it that I was just stretching things to fit my selfish desires when things between Mike and I were still tough?

I knew it seemed like a farfetched story (and after all, I am a writer with a good imagination who knows how to tell a good story) but I didn't think that I could make this story up even if I tried. Later, I found out that I wasn't the one who made it up, but rather Satan, who was playing a deceitful game in my mind for decades. I reflected to my imaginary man and realized that it either seemed like the profile picture of my mentor on his website, or I just really, really wanted to believe that he was the image of a Savior to all my problems. After all, we can convince ourselves of just about anything, and more importantly, so can the enemy.

In the beginning of my journey, I believe that my mentor had a hunch about this imaginary man and asked me why I kept expressing that Mike wasn't the one for me. He asked me this question at least three times before the secret of the imaginary man that I held onto for decades finally came pouring out. The previous visions and voices came into my mind and without thinking I said, "Well, I never told anyone this before, but I think that God told me that there would be someone coming into my life, and that this would be the man of my dreams coming for me." I must admit that I felt a bit pathetic when the words sprang from my lips. I knew that it was far-fetched, and I went through a period when I considered this message to be a Satan attack on my marriage, but I just didn't want to let go of that dream. I really didn't know how to let go of it. No matter how painful it was to have this desire, I did not want anyone to burst my bubble.

It was an awakening when I realized that there was part of me believing that my mentor's profile picture was the image of the man of my dreams. I was confused and had difficulty accepting this new thought of mine. After all, I had prayed for a spiritual mentor, not for my imaginary man. Was I trying to fill my two largest voids at the same time? I still could not deny that my feelings for him did not fall under the category of mentorship by any means, but something about him was extremely attractive to me, and maybe I wasn't quite yet finished chasing my dream.

I allowed time to pass without really considering any of what was happening because I knew that he was a married man. So, I was thinking to myself that my imagination had crossed the line into a lustful sin once again, and coveting was a sin that I never wanted to cross. This was a married man with a family, and I was married with a family, so these thoughts tortured me inside. I thought "Why do I always have to complicate my life?" There was just no way that I was ever going to go into another woman's territory and steal her husband, no matter who I thought he looked like. I came to the decision to let this connection between my imaginary man and my mentor go. Somewhere deep inside, I knew it wasn't right, but I needed to come to grips with it.

I tried everything I could to get the thoughts of my mentor out of my mind. I removed him from my Facebook page multiple times just so that I didn't have to be reminded of him anymore. I pulled back completely from the mentorship/relationship (whatever it was) to continue working on myself and my marriage. This was followed by me calling him to re-start the mentorship again, only to stop it a short while later. I started and stopped so many times that I went around in circles like a dog chasing its tail for months, believing that I had gone completely over the edge of despair with the obvious many problems that remained deep inside.

As I went back and forth through all of this, I thought back to the very first time that I spoke to him on the phone. Remembering the first time that I heard his voice caused an instant spark of something coming alive inside of me. Still, I was left with the visions and a part of my heart still believed that he may have been the man of my dreams. The craziest part of it was that I had never met him, and yet my feelings were so powerful that the miles between us didn't even matter. Meanwhile, during the mentorship, he never revealed anything about himself personally, and so in reality, I knew not much about him at all. My thoughts were all in my own wild and crazy imagination, and I believe now that somehow, he had known about my thoughts, and wanted me to come to the truth about them and my problems.

During this time that I struggled with all of this, I had a sudden sense of a pull on my heart with an overwhelming feeling of love that I had for him. I just started to sing out a sad, sappy love song called, "Hopelessly devoted to you, by Olivia Newton John." It brought me back to the time when I was eleven years old. This was a song I used to sing repeatedly. It was from a movie called "Grease", which is still my all-time favorite movie to this day, but maybe I will get over that too. I decided to watch the video of this song and some of the scenes from the movie Grease that I hadn't seen in a long time.

As I watched the scenes, I was suddenly reminded of the male character that I fell madly in love with as a little girl. He played the role of a street racer and built race car engines. Not surprisingly, Sammy my mentor was also a builder of professional race car engines. The connection was too great for me to ignore. After watching the scenes from the movie my entire insides shook me to the core. I yelled out, "I have been waiting for you all of my life!" Wow, I felt like I knew him before I ever met him. Had I dreamed him right into my life? I desperately needed to find out the truth once and for all.

After confessing to Mike, the truth about these confusing thoughts, he urged me to face reality. Now there was no doubt about it. Still missing my daughter, and desiring to face the truth about Sammy, and what role he had in my life, I made up my mind. There was no question about it. I needed to go to California.

Chapter 39

Miles Between Us

Looking back now, California only represented the "runaway place" in my mind. I struggled with having to accept that Los Angeles was my daughter's temporary new home. I desperately needed to break free from missing her, and realizing California was where she needed to be, I had no other choice than to visit her. California was also my break-away that I thought was so desperately needed from Mike.

It took hard work on my part to accept the long distance between my daughter and I, not just in the distance between New York and LA, but especially a distance still left in our personal relationship. Rather than focusing only on myself, as I had done in the past, I began to focus on supporting her for who she truly was, and not who I expected her to be. I was no longer in the position to be a disciplinary parent to her, but rather to be a mother that loved, accepted, and respected the grown-up decisions that she made for her own life.

With my new perspective at hand, I was no longer judging what I thought she should be doing for me. In the past, this was always an unreasonable expectation of mine that she needed to fill, just so that I could feel loved. If she didn't live up to my expectations, an immediate feeling of rejection would typically leave me wounded and broken apart. A full-fledged war would have broken out inside of me thinking that she didn't really love me. Some examples of my unreasonable expectations were for her to call to me every other day of the week, or to say certain things to me to ease my insecurities. I would have loved for her to have said that she still needed me like every young child needs their mother.

I envisioned her writing a mushy three-page letter explaining just how much she missed me and wanted to come home, until one day I began realizing that maybe underneath it all, I still wanted her to be living her life for me. It was simply a pathetic expectation for her to fill my own personal voids! I was completely dysfunctional as a woman and a mother. It still makes me pause today realizing just how awesome God's love really is as He revealed these truths to me. Once I took this to heart, I was finally on my way to being made whole, and our relationship was open to being completely restored. It was great knowing that I was not hung up on these kind of insecurities in my relationship with her anymore. My love for her was not based on her performance, but rather embraced her for who she truly was on the inside.

Along this journey with God, both of us began understanding the need to live for our own God-given dreams and purposes. As we kept our focus on God, we were discovering the purpose for this season of our lives.

Deciding to travel from New York to Los Angeles was much more complicated for me than for the average person. I had been suffering with vertigo for twenty years, which was always aggravated with altitude changes. For years, I had difficulty with balance and dizziness, feeling like I had permanent seasickness. Just the thought of air travel made me cringe with the concern of re-aggravating my condition. It had been over two decades since I had flown in a plane, and I was determined that my faith was stronger than any fears I had about the vertigo, so I decided to take a short flight to Boston to wet my feet for the long flight to California. With the courage that God had given me, I was able to take this short flight without any fear. Nevertheless, I wound up having a severe vertigo attack with every altitude change the plane made. The entire flight became a complete disaster, but I was not fooled by Satan's tactics because I knew God was working on a victory flight in my future. After finally landing, I knew for sure that the only way I would get to California at this time was to drive across the country. I was not about to allow anything to stop me from getting there.

In October of 2015, Mike and I began our trip across the country, even though our future together was once again a rocky road of uncertainty. As we crossed over each state line there were so many amazing sights that I had only dreamed of seeing. I realized just how beautiful this country really was. Everything from corn to cow country, and into the Rocky Mountains were breath taking. This trip was as adventurous as it gets for me, but unlike our river rafting and camping adventures, we stayed in the most luxurious resorts from beginning to end. We overlooked the city lights from the heights of hotel penthouses, and then retreated to the highest peaks of the mountain resorts. This was the kind of adventure that I had always dreamed of having, and yet, because Mike was driving me across the country so I could find out certain truths about myself, and the possibility of not returning to a life with him, the intimacy that such a trip should have had was sadly missing.

Regardless of our rocky relationship, Mike planned every morsel of this trip for me, and by now he knew me well enough to know what I'd like, and how to choose just the right places. After long days of driving, we dined at the very best and romantic restaurants. Without a doubt, this was the greatest trip that we had ever been on with one major exception. I had not yet come to my senses and was still on the run, in complete denial about it. Leading up to this trip, it was like a switch inside of me just shut me off from Mike, and I made it clear to him that I might be leaving him. I thought this was a one-way farewell trip. I told him that I was not certain if I would ever return to him again.

I thought that my new life may have belonged in California because this was the direction my imagination seemed to be heading me towards. I had even alluded to Mike the fact that being together with the love of my life (my mentor), and doing ministry work, was my dream. I absolutely cannot even imagine how tragically hurt Mike must have been that I was leaving him once again, but he remained truly faithful

225

... and loved me, even when I didn't love him in return. Deep down, I was feeling so guilty for treating him in a way that no man should have ever been treated by his so called "wife". I was in absolute denial that I was still on the run, searching for my dream lover.

I told myself it was different for me this time than when I had also separated from him years ago because I believed that God was calling me to go. I thought this was a mission to bring me together with the "man of my dreams" but, since I still was not sure of what exactly God's plans were, I was not about to be presumptuous. All this time, Mike knew this was not God's plan, and made sure he left the door open for my return. I know for most, it sounds crazy that he would plan this amazing trip across country trying to woo me before seeing me off, but the whole time he was already onto my tricks and was one step ahead of me. He also knew where I was going was safe and trusted that God had a plan. He wanted to love me for as much time as I gave him, and this trip eventually wound up proving his unconditional love to me more so than ever before.

I found myself once again fighting this battle inside of me, knowing deep down just how wrong it was to separate from my husband (again), but on the other hand, I also knew that God had a plan. I just wasn't seeing it yet. In my heart, I realized that I still must've been an unstable woman, and I needed serious help! I also knew that Mike became aware that he alone could not help me see the truth about myself until I was ready. He was holding on to the faith that God was lining everything up, so that one day I would. Ultimately, he knew that he needed to step back and let me depart. It was the only way he told me that I would ever discover what I really wanted.

When I think back, it astounds me how much faith he had to have to watch the love of his life leave him once again. This time he did not resist my desire to run. Instead, he encouraged me to go. This was my decision that I would have to live with once and for all, and whatever kind of a mess that I made of my life, I would have to one day clean it all up. I thought, "If it turned out that I was wrong, and the grass wasn't greener on the other side, I would only have myself to blame."

After five days on the road, and the sighting of the first palm tree, we were finally getting closer to our destination. As we approached the Los Angeles signs, it seemed surreal that we drove across the entire country without a hitch. God brought us over 3,000 miles so quickly, it seemed as if it was just around the corner. We arrived late on a Sunday night. I couldn't wait to join my daughter in the adventures of her new life, and to finally meet with my "mentor/soulmate". I wasn't sure which one of these two he was anymore. I was grateful and wanted to at least thank him personally for all he had done for my daughter, while my conscience was screaming out to me that my romantic feelings for him were wrong.

Although my daughter had been in the safety of his mentorship for nearly two years, and there are no words that could have ever expressed our thankfulness to him for saving her life from the uncertainty of the streets, I was still living in this dreamland of denial about my reasons for going there in the first place. Up until this point, I imagined that he was a faraway saint that I was in love with, who just happened to be taking care of my daughter while I couldn't. He took her out of harm's way and into the life that she had always dreamed of having. As hard as this was for me at first to imagine her life without me, deep down, I was ever so grateful that she finally had a place to call home and a life of her own pursuing God.

On the day we arrived, Mike and I met with Sammy for the first time. Talk about an awkward moment! There I was, with this big secretive life, planning to leave my husband for this man, when a sudden tide of unresolved emotions hit me like a brick. There was suddenly something strange about all this to me. With the pressure of my own convictions bearing down on me, I knew everything I had believed was suddenly in a total whirlwind. I had no idea at the time how to even express the anger that I was suddenly feeling towards Sammy, as if it were all his fault that I had gone a bit crazy. I didn't even understand why I was feeling this uncomfortable rage inside of me, except that I felt completely foolish for believing that he was my Mr. Right! For some reason, I felt like I was led right into this great big trap on purpose. Boy was I ever such a fool! He knew how I felt about him because I had already expressed it to him, and there he was acting like a stranger to me, or I wondered if that was all in my imagination too?

After my whirlwind of emotions began to simmer down, my daughter and her music team sat together to sing her new song for us, but as she sang her song, I was completely unable to focus on it. I was still trying to figure out what exactly was going on with my life! I began asking myself what my honest reasons were for being in California. I felt like I was in a complete trance, as if my life was passing before me. I realized that part of my reasons for being there were for the craziest ideas that I ever had in my life, and yet this was somehow so typical for me by this point to be running away trying to escape from somewhere or someone. I wondered why I was always running from or to something bouncing around like a ping pong ball.

As I began to snap myself out of this thick brain fog, I was trying to listen to what was supposed to be one of the most beautiful moments of my life, which was listening to my daughter sing her inspiring new song. About halfway through her song, I began realizing how important this moment was for her, and how I didn't want to ruin it. I did everything I could to look like I was moved by her song, but my guess was that it came off as a bit odd because of my own confusion about where I was and why.

Mike had to fly back home the next day and return to work. The thoughts of him leaving began creeping in and hit me hard. I had a few thoughts that I wanted to run again, but right back into his arms. I felt like a completely insane woman, but I knew I needed to stop running and this was it! I was going to get to the bottom of this behavior of mine and out of this never-ending marathon. Both my husband and I knew in our hearts that there was a hard lesson to be learned while I was there. So, we made our way to the airport and said our last "Goodbye."

As soon as he let go of me, there was an instant feeling of heartache tearing me up inside. I felt that this was the real moment of truth. It was the one where I had pictured nothing but freedom in my mind. This was my destination, the one that I always dreamed of, but as Mike turned away, something inside of me never wanted to let go. There are really no words to express my emotions as my entire life with him flashed before my eyes, and how much of my own strength it took to try to bury the thoughts of my life without him. If all of this didn't hit me hard enough, what was about to happen over the next few months was going to be far worse.

The first day without Mike sort of felt like my childhood and the first day of school. I was uneasy and had no idea what was in store for my life next. I would spend the next several months unveiling the state of my poor sickened soul. I was led around to meet everyone associated with Sammy and his ministry who was actually "supposed" to be there. I quickly hit another reality check when I met his wife ... and his children. I greeted her with a big phony smile. There was a sudden feeling as if a cat fight was about to break out. I gathered that she somehow already had an idea about my feelings for her husband. My life seemed to always get me into a jam. I began wondering just how wrong I was for being there away from Mike, and that maybe my life back home was not so bad after all.

Things were once again beginning to change inside of me. What an awakening this was turning out to be. I began asking myself questions like "What in the world was I doing here, and how did I always get myself into these crazy situations?", and "How would I ever write a book about being a holy Christian woman after this?" My life was turning into a dramatic episode of a dreary soap opera.

After a long day of being out of my element and into these new challenges, I went to Sammy's house, where I was going to settle into the lovely guestroom. Although I was grateful for a place to stay, after meeting his wife I was obviously uneasy about my decision to be there, especially without Mike. It was apparent his wife didn't seem to welcome me in at first, but graciously allowed it, as they were always housing anyone in need as part of his ministry. I felt so lonely and insecure in the new surroundings. Regardless, I knew that I had to make the best of it while I was there, and I honestly did want to reconnect with my daughter in her new life somehow.

I had a lot of time to think about things while I was there, and I wanted to start all over again by being honest with everyone in my life. I began thinking of his wife and how she must have felt threatened by my dishonest motives. The only way that I knew how to change the awkward conflict between myself, and his wife was to attempt making peace with her, although this was not what my selfish side really wanted to do. However, I sensed that God wanted me to, and this was my first instruction while I was there.

The decision to please God (instead of myself) was the first mission at hand. As the month progressed, I did everything possible to prove to her that I was trustworthy. I respected their family above everything else, and finally stopped my fantasies about her husband. As soon as the reality hit me that they were a family, I literally dropped my dream like a hot potato.

Of all the places in the world that I could have made such a decision, it was in a disgusting porta potty that I decided to give up this selfish dream once and for all. God was having quite a chat with me in this smelly, forsaken place of germs. I wondered for a moment, "Was this God's way of showing me some kind of sign that my choices in life really stunk?" Maybe so. Regardless of anyone else, all I could think about while holding my nose from the bad smell, was what in the world made me believe that this man was "The One" for me? I knew that he was married, but I guess I was hoping he wasn't. To be honest, maybe I was hoping that he was unhappily married just as I seemed to be.

The truth about my evil intentions went straight into my heart and hurt like hell. I was completely ashamed of myself when I saw his family together. I had no idea what to think anymore ... other than to try not to. Later, I learned that his family had obviously been threatened with other lustful women, just like me! They tried to wreck their whole world and interfere with their personal lives with nothing more than their selfish lustful desires, trying to hunt down this man. I did not want to wreck anyone else's life, but wherever I went, I surely seemed to. I wanted to curl up in a ball and hide myself forever for believing that this married man was the man of my dreams. They had three beautiful children, and I fell in love with each of them. They were honestly the wisest and most beautiful children that I had ever met. After a while, I enjoyed most of my days spending time with them.

With all the harsh realities staring me in the face, and bearing down on my conscience, I couldn't dream my dream anymore without knowing how deceived I really was, and what a destructive path I was on. I absolutely hated living with anymore secrets inside of me. It seemed no matter where I went there was nothing but my secrets following me. I couldn't win no matter how I spun it in my mind. I couldn't ever seem to figure out the underlying problem that I was having. Somewhere in the back of my mind however, I was just beginning to recognize that my thoughts were delusional. I tried so hard to stand on my own two feet, and ground myself in the Lord, but for the first time since my journey with God began, I felt nothing but miles between us. The harsh reality finally hit me, that for most of my life, I had only identified myself in men, and it was painful for me to admit it. Most of the time, it wasn't really love at all, but was just my lust for someone else to fill my entire world of difficulties, trying to make me feel good about myself. I knew by this point I had to go back to square one, and rely on God for my identity, and no one else.

This trip was so far off from what I had envisioned it would be. I basically went there to live my dream life and wound up feeling like a great big lost and pathetic fool. It was so painful for me because I didn't even understand how I wound up in this lost place all over again. I felt horribly misled down this reoccurring broken road.

The good news was that I was finally coming out of this love trance, and I realized that I had violated some major boundaries with just about everyone in my life. I will confess that the very first moment I spent alone with Sammy, I got close and looked deep into his eyes. The next thing I knew, I was telling him how I was in love with him! This feeling was very real for me, but my words meant nothing to him. I pictured myself driving down a one-way street with a giant sign staring me straight in the face that was shouting, **"WRONG WAY!"** I was speechless (for once). I thought "What have I done now?" I didn't have any answers at the time, except by the look on his face, he made it clear that he was not in love with me. Then he reached out to pray over my desperate soul. It was a surreal moment, like this couldn't really be happening to me. It may go down in history as one of the most awkward moments in a woman's life. Instantly, there was a stab of rejection piercing straight through my heart like an arrow. In this very moment, I blamed God that I believed in any of my heart's desires as it says in Psalm 37:4, but I twisted this scripture to serve my own purely evil and selfish desires.

Looking back, I understood that I was led right up to this very moment to finally understand the depths of my problem. I realized that I was a runner, a prodigal, and a woman who was on a mission to destroy everyone's lives, including my own. I finally knew why Shannon's runaway hit me so hard, as it only reflected my own desire to always run from my problems.

Mike had driven over 3,000 miles and ACROSS THE ENTIRE COUNTRY knowing full and well it was for me to finally meet "The One", hoping that I would suddenly come to my senses and find out that he wasn't. I realized that Satan sure can make up a good story, and it takes discernment to finally become aware of his ugly, deceitful lies.

I realize now that my imaginary man was a delusion that morphed into a reality designed to destroy me and my marriage. It always gave me an excuse to escape from my own reality instead of working on my problems. I came to understand that this imaginary man was at the core of the problem in my marriage and was the major roadblock standing between myself and my husband. I would never underestimate Satan's relentlessness ever again. He did whatever he could to trip me up, but he knew that his control over me was finished.

Once I grasped that I was caught in this web of lies, the truth had become clear to me. It wasn't long before I heard the soft whisper from God (a few times) asking me to go back home. I decided to start packing my bags and called Mike to let him know that I was ready to return and reconcile. He asked me

235

if I was certain of this decision. Once and for all I knew I finally was done running. It was settled in my mind, and I wanted nothing more than to love my husband forevermore. I realized just how bizarre my life had been, but I said to myself, "don't worry", because one day I would look back at our time apart, knowing the miles between us led me back home.

Chapter 40

Welcome Home

I will never forget the day when I arrived home and Mike led me through the front door. There were colorful balloons, and handmade welcome signs that adorned the living room walls. My return home was an incredible celebration of love. I imagined him preparing for my homecoming for several days before I arrived. I could see the joy shine through the wonderful colors on the posters, giving me the comfort that I longed for. I was grateful to be back where I knew I belonged.

Mike had finally witnessed one of the greatest miracles of all, the return of a completely different woman. I was the kind of wife he was waiting for all along. What once was nothing but a bitter and confused woman, was now a wife filled with a heart to discover a true love for her husband. While I was gone, he didn't grow bitter or fall apart without me. He kept his heart pure and full of hope, ready to forgive, and lived for the Lord. He never spoke of divorce, no matter what the circumstances were, but he knew he needed to let go, step back, and allow God to work all things for good. He was going to hold on and never give up on me, even when our lives were caving in. He knew there was too much at stake and standing for what he believed in was worth it in the end. It was in fact my husband's stand that played a vital role which helped lead to my deliverance. It took him great faith not to enable my self-destruction in any way. He dealt with me in a manner that would draw me back to him. His love shined through darkness and made a way for me to see the truth I needed.

Despite my lack of faith, he was going to stand and fight for me. Deep within his heart, he knew nothing could replace his one and only. During the toughest times, he grew closer to God and stronger in faith. He mastered his great test of trials and tribulations. He stood fast, hoped against hope, believed beyond belief, and rarely wavered. He believed the outcome would fulfill his desire for our complete restoration. He learned what it meant to be still while waiting for my return. He trusted that God would help him in whatever he needed to do to help me find what was in my best interest, regardless of what would happen to him or our relationship. He had persevered in walking his test of faith and was rewarded with his dream come true when I returned to him.

It was quite a long road, but the many struggles I endured led to a true freedom, where Christ had set me free from the torment of sin. I was faced with important decisions to make. It was in the decision to embrace my beloved family, to put their needs above my own. It meant my concern for my family's happiness was above my own, it meant personal sacrifice, and self-denial. Even after everything I had tortured Mike with, crossing those lines that should have never been crossed, making him endure all the horrible things I had said and done, things he never dreamed I would ever do, he had only the look of unconditional love in his eyes. He made me feel that I owed him nothing at all.

I was misled with the sinful idea that my lovers might be the answer to my needs, so I pursued them with an obsession. I threw off the appearance of marriage for my deluded passions, somehow believing I could get someone better than my husband. The kind of love that I desired, however, could only be found in the living God. Mike's example of genuine love for me was a replica of God's faithful love for His Bride. I am sure however, that Mike never imagined marrying a wife who would utterly reject and betray him, and yet he gave everything he had from his heart in pursuit of me. Although in his suffering, he had briefly questioned God as to whether he should continue this path of love, his mind immediately jumped from his situation to a deeper understanding of God's faithful love for us.

Even though I had separated from him, he made certain that he made the proper provisions for me. He knew no one else would care for me like he did. God reminded me repeatedly of how deeply he cared for me while I was miles away from him. I knew deep down that no one else on earth could bestow this kind of grace or mercy towards me. Even though I was committed to my own path of selfish desires and looked everywhere else to be fulfilled, he was committed to be an image of the Divine Husband. He knew it was impossible to satisfy my lusts, but he kept loving me, imploring me to turn away from my selfish desires and find the true desire for our marital love. Finally, I understood the truth about my sinful and wayward life. I wanted nothing more than to ask for his forgiveness, to say that I was genuinely sorry for all the hurt I caused and show my love for him. This was truly a moment of forgiveness in the hopes of a new beginning, and no sooner was he by my side to bring me back home.

Coming back with all my heart was long awaited, and I knew that it would be one of the greatest love stories ever told. This kind of love did not come without a battle, but we chose to love "us" with a passionate, faithful love, forevermore. It was a time for great celebration, laughter, and tears of joy. All we ever hoped for was found, knowing that nothing could ever tear us apart. Even when there were miles between us, and damage that nearly cost us everything, nothing was too hard for God to make a way for my welcome home.

Chapter 41

Between Mother and Daughter

It has been nearly seven years since that tragic day when our family's lives had fallen apart. The day of my daughter Shannon's runaway will always be a symbol of just how lost we once were. Although many miles stood between us, I held onto my faith, knowing God would give us back stolen time, and everything we were robbed of in our hearts. While she was gone, God's promise to me remained, that she would return home indefinitely someday.

The first few years following my return home were not easy. My father, who was one of the only people on earth who really knew me, had become terminally ill. We were always kindred spirits, with similarities between us, unlike anyone else. We could just look into each other's eyes and know what we were thinking. We could laugh at the silliest things together that no one else would. We appreciated much of the same things in life and knew how to enjoy time with one another. He was truly my hero, my confidant, and one who I could trust and count on when I asked for advice. For example, when I asked him years ago what I should do about my unsatisfying marriage, he said to me, "divorce is not an option". I was fuming at him for that advice, but it was all he needed to say. During the toughest times in our marriage, his words rang truth in my ears. It turns out those very words had the power to save my marriage. Instead of bailing out, we found better solutions, God's solutions.

During the time of my father's declining health, Shannon had come back from California for a visit. We spent time with my father in the hospital, and we prayed together. On the next to last day of his life on earth, we were moved to sing Shannon's new song called "Hold On" to him. I knew it was one of the most special moments of his life, and of ours too. Although his face was covered with an oxygen mask and could barely move, one of his fingers managed to wave up and down to the sound of us singing her song. The other patient that was sharing the room with my father had suddenly jumped out of his bed, pulled his curtain back, and yelled with excitement, "I have never heard anything like this before, it is so beautiful!" We paused for a moment and smiled at him, then we continued to sing for them both. I knew God was ever so present with us. Joy had filled all our hearts in the hospital room that day, even though our eyes could only see deathly sickness. I realized that the encouraging power of her song healed the brokenness in people. I know the miracles that occurred that day would have never happened if both of our hearts had not already changed.

When we were finally about to leave the room, I noticed my father gasping for air, but I softly whispered in his ear, "Dad, quit telling yourself you can't breathe. I want to see that mask off your face tomorrow!" The next day when we walked into his room, he was sitting up in the chair without the mask and breathing perfectly fine. It was truly yet another miracle! We spent the afternoon listening to the animated stories he told us about his childhood. I had to keep blinking at the sight of him because I was astounded that he was not the same man we had left just the day before. Yet somehow, deep down inside, I knew it was his last day with us as God's gift. It was our final chance to listen to him. Maybe he knew something too.

He seemed to be in a euphoric state, unaware of his condition. He didn't want to eat or drink anything, but only desired that we listen to him. At one point, I felt as if I were in a fog, and became unable to listen to him intently. It didn't take long before he caught me not hearing what he was saying. He was very annoyed with me for not being mentally present, and it was so unlike him to demand anyone's attention. It led me to believe that he knew just how little time we had left together, and how Satan was trying to steal my attention thinking about things that really didn't matter as much as listening to my father that day. He was trying to steal the final moments we had together.

It was a complete nightmare for me watching him wither away over his last few years. He was in and out of the hospital so many times, and it was taking a toll on all of us. My father was a brave man, and a fighter who refused to complain right up to the end. He didn't want to leave us, but the day after his story telling, it was over. He left us to be with the Lord, but I am so grateful for the time I had with him over my life. I only wished it were longer. There are still days that I miss him so much it hurts, but I know that while he was here on earth, the changes he witnessed in both Shannon, and I helped convince him that Jesus was our Lord and Savior. He had become a believer in Christ at nearly eighty years old. I can rest assured now, knowing he is with our heavenly Father, that we will rejoice when we see him again.

The day after Shannon had gone back to California, my father passed away. I didn't want her to leave. I was tired of goodbyes by this point, and I knew his final days were upon us. I wanted her there, but for some reason, I believe she always wanted to remember us together, praying with him, singing to him, and listening to his stories as her final goodbye to her grandfather. I had to face the next week saying goodbye to my father by preparing his eulogy. As I stood on the podium reading it the night of my father's wake, I paused for a moment only to see the tears pouring from my son's eyes. I nearly crumbled but went on reading and said my final goodbye. I don't think there was a single dry eye in the room hearing about what a wonderfully dedicated man he was to so many people, especially to my mother for over sixty years.

The next few weeks were a complete blur, but the one thing I knew for certain was that the time Shannon and I spent with my father became some of the most heartfelt moments we had ever shared. The two of us, during this very painful time, were finally beginning to have the kind of relationship that I always dreamed should happen between mother and daughter.

Chapter 42

Together at Last

It was a Saturday afternoon, our twenty ninth wedding anniversary, when the phone rang. Mike answered, it was Shannon's voice on speaker phone. We said our usual hello and chatted for a while before she made the announcement. She was finally coming back home! It didn't sink in at first. We just thought she was coming home for another visit, but this time, she made it clear that it was for an indefinite amount of time. She was busy packing all her things and leaving California to come home to New York. We had to ask her a few times because we were so surprised by the news. We asked her again to be sure we understood, "How long are you coming back for?" She said, "I have a one-way ticket to New York." Halleluiah! This was the moment we had been patiently waiting for... she's finally coming back home!

It was just wonderful knowing our time together wouldn't only be for a short visit. Her time away over the past years felt like an eternity. It was almost seven years since she had run away, and we tried to keep our hearts guarded from the fact that we missed her so. I couldn't allow myself to think about it for too long, about how much I missed her, and how cheated I felt for the way she had left us. I never dreamed my child would run away or could have ever foretold the tragedy and personal growth that awaited us. It all seemed like a bad dream that I had finally woken up from.

We looked forward to the big homecoming day with anticipation. It was a strange time though. The world was in the middle of a devastating pandemic that struck many to the core. We had been in quarantine and going out into public seemed a thing of the past. Most of us spent our time at home, and when we went out into public, we wore masks. I was so glad that my father missed all this crazy mess. It seemed the world stopped turning and nothing was the way it used to be. We missed all our family and the holidays together. We didn't go out for dinners, or really do anything outside of our own home except for getting the necessities. People stayed at home and feared for their lives for years. Hundreds of thousands of people were dead from the virus and there was still no end in sight, but during this terrible time, we managed to find joy.

The day finally arrived to pick up Shannon at the airport. I could hardly wait! When we pulled into the terminal, we saw her with HUGE pieces of luggage packed tightly containing every one of her belongings. There wasn't any time for long hugs at this point. We just needed to get her and her things into the truck as quickly as possible to minimize our contact time with the crowd.

The media had scared most people half to death concerning the pandemic, and most wanted nothing to do with the outside world. I could not imagine going through this era without knowing that I am a child of God and know that I am going to heaven in the end. I am so glad that I know the truth about who I am, and how I will be spending eternity with Jesus. We do not focus on the media, and we have not allowed anyone to strike fear into us, nor have we succumbed to the fears that make one stop living their life. Our lives have never been more rewarding, as the entire world seems to be in a constant state of depression and sheer panic. It has never been more apparent that we are separate from many others in the world. As Christians, we separate from the world's emphasis on negativity, and instead focus on our relationship with God.

When I finally saw Shannon, I was overwhelmed with sheer excitement. Once Mike hoisted her stuff up into the truck, we drove straight to our vacation home in Pennsylvania. My mother had been living with us in New York for nine months since my father had passed away. She had to sell her house, so we wanted to quarantine Shannon away from my mother for any possibility of passing on the virus to her. While we spent the next two weeks together in Pennsylvania, we never laughed so hard just being goofy and light-hearted. That same week, my mother moved out of our house in New York and into her new apartment. Two weeks later, we brought Shannon back to New York to reunite with her brother Connor.

Thanksgiving was upon us, and we had a lot to be grateful for! The holidays were like some of the old times with Shannon being home. It was a time to truly enjoy one another and make up for all the time we had lost. It was time to rebuild our trust for one another and keep building on our growing relationship. I was completely happy and deeply overjoyed! Words just cannot describe how blessed I felt as a mother, being able to do all the mother/daughter things together that God had planned for us. Even the everyday little things we did together brought me so much happiness. We walked together, cooked together, laughed together, worshipped together, shopped together, and honestly learned how to get along. For once, we had deep and meaningful conversations about what really mattered in our lives. Our changing relationship was no longer led by our selfish desires, as both of us learned how to finally love unconditionally.

After some time, I finally asked her what made her return home to us. Ironically, she said she heard God say, "Go Home" just as I had heard when I was in California. She was living for her dream life, writing songs and singing, as well as being a part of ministry, but she dropped it all because she knew that God wanted her to come home to spend time with family. It was time to do the things together that we should have done long ago. It was obvious that God made choosing the responsibilities of our family the top priority, and sacrifice was necessary. A healed family was more important to all of us than anything else. I can't say that I know for sure what God's plans are for our future, but for now we are completely content just being together.

Five months after Shannon moved back home to New York, we decided to move full time to our secondary home in

Pennsylvania. It was another transition for her to move again, but we had to move on, and into the next chapter of our lives. God had led us to this move for many reasons. The pandemic allowed us to re-evaluate our lives and determine what was most important. Selling our house in New York and cutting Mike's workdays from six per week down to three, was the solution. It afforded us the precious element that was missing for so long- more time together. Our lives were honestly leading up to this for some time anyway. We needed a change from the fast-paced life that New York would have only kept us in. We were finally free from the idea of living like the rest of the world. While we never were concerned with "keeping up with the Jones' ", too many people around us in New York were, and it just helped direct where we wanted to live. We desired a simpler life in the country, being able to do things in nature, enjoying the outdoors, and especially Mike's ability to finally kick-back and relax. As he continues to overcome his intense work drive that added to our marital problems for years, and we spend more relaxed time together, we are better able to communicate and meet each other's needs. Our relationship is not perfect but thriving at last.

God's timing was perfect because we sold our home at the height of a seller's market and tripled our initial investment, paying off our debts, and allowing Mike to semi-retire. No more mortgages, car payments, credit cards, high tax rates, high food and grocery bills, utility bills, or large purchases that kept us spending more than what we made each month. We learned that living up to what you can afford, or above it, is not the kind of living we were interested in anymore. For the first time in a long time, we were able to save more money than we were spending.

It is an entirely new way of life for us. We are free to pursue more interests and spend our days doing the things we enjoy. We have discovered new talents, explored new ideas, and most importantly, nurtured our relationships. Each of us are finding a deeper, personal fulfillment and know we serve a greater purpose. The sky is the limit with God in the center of our everyday lives. We are finally as they say," Living the dream", and together we have become a family once again.

Chapter 43

When I Said," I Do"

After I had returned home to my husband, I felt like a dog with its tail between its legs. A part of me wanted to force my way past the feeling of failure, and grief, but I knew this was a time for healing. I realized it wasn't going to be an easy road ahead. I knew it was going to be painful, exhausting, and humbling at times.

Facing the harsh reality of my romance addiction was beyond words. The addiction was a sad attempt to avoid the tragic state of my inner chaos. I knew that trying to numb the pain of how worthless, empty, or troubled I felt inside, romance was not the solution I was looking for. I had to face reality about the detestable things that I had done because of what I was secretly believing. Confronting all my sinful behaviors, and becoming honest with myself, was the only way out of my misery.

The more that I pursued God for my personal healing, the more in depth my understanding became about my behaviors. As they surfaced, I realized that I wound up with an obsessive passion for lust as some pathetic way of trying to feel loved. I didn't know the difference between love and lust. This evil spirit swept through my life with empty promises and left me surrendering my sexual purity. I had to go down every gloomy detail of loss from my past to allow God to make a different path for my future.

My stomach turned as I looked back over the dysfunctional behaviors of my life. I analyzed myself from every low point and saw the sad struggles of the lost woman I had become. My brokenness was the continuation of many generations in my family who had suffered the great loss of who they truly were. They were an example of those who refused to take full responsibility for their identity, and instead passively went through their lives with frustration. The lies that I was believing about myself, or telling myself daily, was an ignorance of the truth. The dysfunction of those whom I had looked up to in the past had only helped to deplete me of having an accurate image of my own identity.

Passiveness, and a lack of discipline, was the culprit of idleness in my life. I was always looking for someone else to take responsibility for my own sense of fulfillment. This type of behavior is what I learned as "normal" growing up as a child. I expected my world of relationships to become my source of inner joy and happiness. Trying to define myself in them had only failed me to no end. With a world of addictive relationships at my fingertips, my life stood still.

I never discovered who I truly was, and falsely believed that I had to surrender myself in ways that only brought shame, sorrow, and discontentment. I never developed a relationship with God to understand what a healthy, well-balanced relationship was with myself ... or anyone else.

Going back in time with my self-analysis enabled me to understand my dire need for attracting the attention of other men at any cost. At a young age, I began identifying myself through sexual immorality, trying to attach myself to boys, and later to men, all of whom did not love me. I had no idea of the depth that this sinful sexual expression had traveled throughout my life until I hit rock bottom. The more that I searched for myself in men, the more lost I was.

The world normalized fornication. I never remembered being taught to be sexually pure for marriage. I think it was just expected of me from my parents, without it ever being spoken, until it was too late. Somewhere deep down though, it was my desire to wait for the man that I married, but I was pressured into having sex with nothing but empty promises. I had no idea who I was or what the truth was for my life without God, but today I do. Sexual immorality was a sin that I had committed against my own body, and the results were even more devastating when I finally realized it had torn my marriage apart. It took years to personally heal from the wounds of my sexual sin. It took several more years for both my husband and I to heal together, and for our marriage to be truly restored.

The bible is clear that sex was created to be enjoyed between one man and one woman who are in a covenant marriage until one of them dies (Matthew 19:6). Sexuality is God's sacred wedding gift that I abused. Any expression of sexual activity outside the parameters of a marriage constitutes as adultery.

I did not honor God, who created marriage in its institution of sacredness. It wasn't until I repented and received His forgiveness that I was cleansed of my impurities. My old nature was put to death. I was no longer that lost woman who was unfit for marriage.

It would have seemed easier in the worst of our marital struggles to cut our losses and part ways like so many married people do. If we kept an account of all the hurt and disappointment, we could have been divorced a million times over. There were decades of pain so deep it seemed we had all the evidence we needed to conclude we were better off divorced, but it was the evidence of our faith that began telling another story. Every trial of pain made us turn to God for the hope we needed to spend the rest of our lives together. Throughout every hardship, we would need to search our hearts for the kind of unconditional love that God provides for us. We learned there would always be a deeper form of love between us after genuine repentance and the offering of forgiveness.

Just as sin had separated me from God, it had separated me from true myself (my identity in Christ), and from Mike. The more I attempted to sever from God's plans for the permanence of our covenant marriage, the more I realized that it wasn't working. I would have only spent the rest of my life regretting a divorce if I had not obeyed the truth. God's written word is clear on marriage being permanent as it says in Mark 10:9, "What therefore God has joined together, let not man separate."

I had been on the fence about whether to stay in my marriage for years, but I finally realized the problems I was having in our relationship were really the problems I was having with myself. The conflicts that were inside of me were the same conflicts that surrounded me. These problems were an absence of my own inner peace and joy.

Trying to demand my own way in the relationship only tormented both of us. I became argumentative, bitter, and resentful of Mike, until I finally reached a point where I had to get honest with myself. Whatever I was doing on my behalf was only hurting our relationship and causing me personal misery. It was time that I stopped expecting him to change, and instead, change the many things about myself I had ignored in the past. God showed me that I had never properly communicated my needs to my husband, and this lack of responsibility on my part was a major problem in our marriage.

Simple problems between us had become HUGE because proper communication was a foreign language to me. No matter how selfishly demanding I was in the attempts to get what I needed or wanted, it never changed a thing. In fact, it only made matters far worse than before. It was disastrous when I tried to control things I could not. My mistake was taking matters into my own hands, rather than using biblical discernment and trusting God. I learned that true love must not insist on its own selfish way, but rather insist on God's way.

The more that I put my faith in God, the more I changed, and the more I realized that I needed restoration in all my relationships. I realized that committing to our marriage and making the best of the good things we have in our relationship was the best way to heal my own discontentment. As I grew to love my everyday life with Mike, the relationship finally healed. It came to a new place of trust, honesty, and intimacy. It was a sheer victory to be able to communicate from a place of love, rather than from a place of unrighteous judgement, blaming, or bashing my way into battles with him. The drama scenes were finally over.

We began to address what we both needed in the relationship. When I found myself expressing my needs openly to him, and he finally understood them, there was an enormous sense of relief. We were fully immersed in our relationship, fostering trust, and creating a sense of security and intimacy that was never there before. We were finally being accountable, and consistently followed through with not just our words, but our actions. Together, we were moving forward for the common goal of a healthy relationship.

When my daughter ran away, and I hit rock bottom, I realized that I was lost without direction or purpose for my life. This was the day I knew I could no longer go on being this woman who relied on her family for her only sense of worth. As I placed my identity in Christ, it became a true state of inner healing. As I adhered to God's commands with all my heart, it changed the meaning of my life and the way that I related to my family. I was no longer pursuing an unfulfilling path that only led to destruction and betrayal.

Going to California only helped me to recognize that I was a runner, a prodigal, and was on a mission to destroy my family's lives. Coming back home helped me to realize there were no longer any secret desires lurking around in the background of my mind. It was quite a heavy blow when I realized my imaginary man was just a lie, as so much of my previous life was also. Now the lies were finally broken and were replaced by the truth. I was made known of my identity as a beloved daughter of the Almighty God. I was no longer feeling like I was a million miles away from God. Letting go of the wrong things in my life brought healing to all my relationships.

Our lives today are not perfect by any means. Both of us have our faults, and while some days seem harder than others, those days are becoming few and far between. When they do occur, the challenges now give way for an opportunity to admit there was a problem to solve. I never wanted to just co-exist in a marriage and settle for less than my true heart's desires. I now know that if I am having a problem, I need to address it with biblical wisdom. I believe there will always be solutions to our problems when we do things God's way.

We are now continually making honest efforts to take responsibility for our mistakes to create positive outcomes. We took many steps to rebuild a seemingly hopeless marriage, making it everything we ever wanted and more, but the foundation for our success was to be faithful and obedient to God, and true to our marital vows, remaining in the covenant of marriage until death do us part.

When I walked down the aisle on my wedding day, I was not prepared for marriage. I could not handle all that was ahead of me or contribute to a healthy relationship. I knew it wasn't supposed to be this way, and as I allowed God to work on renewing my heart and soul, I overcame my struggles of bitterness, anger, resentment, and selfishness. My values were completely renewed. I grew to finally know myself and what really matters. I am now able to look past the things that I let annoy me in the past. I truly admire Mike's strong points now and pray for him in his weaknesses. I have learned to compromise and give up certain things to reach a place of understanding. Marriage isn't just about me anymore, as I now consider my husband's needs above my own. I have more than just my own singular happiness at heart.

I have faced reality head-on and am no longer living in my dysfunctional ideal fantasy of marriage. I no longer yearn for attention from other men or live a secret life anymore. My mind no longer wonders if the grass is greener on the other side. My favorite times are now being content with affectionately spending time together with Mike.

As I have shifted my focus from my husband to God as the source of my satisfaction, it has alleviated a tremendous burden on him. I am no longer trying to manipulate or change him in any way. I have become a respectful and

259

submissive wife. I have learned how to handle finances honestly and no longer have secret debts. I accept our differences, knowing we are both a part of the same body in Christ. I have discovered my own personal stability by persevering through the problems that arise. I have developed patience and endurance during troubled times and now trust in God's promises over any circumstances. I have learned to hold on, despite the seemingly insurmountable number of problems that life can sometimes bring about.

Once I knew that by the grace of God, I could let go of everything in my past, a major shift took place inside of me. It was a new beginning that gave birth to romance, and rekindled love for my husband. I was once a lost woman, but in my moments of solitude and prayer, I was faced with one of the most important decisions of my life. I knew the bridge between us was about to crumble, but I took one final leap of faith, and chose the road home. At last, I have finally surrendered my heart and come to know what forever meant when I said, "I Do".

Chapter 44

Come Back Home

Wouldn't it be a dream come true for everyone to have their marriage and family restored? What if every marriage and family was the kind that was thriving, where all members were doing their own part and working towards their common goals? I've come to realize this isn't always how it works, and I believe more commonly this isn't the way most of us experience marriage or family life in our everyday lives. My journey has led me to believe that love becomes much more complicated than any of us have knowingly signed up for on our wedding day or on the day our first child is born.

Having unrealistic expectations of the ones we love can play a major role in these complications. Looking back over the years with God's insight allowed me to realize that so many of my previous troubles turned out to be the result of my own unrealistic expectations of others.

I expected others to live my life for me, for Mike and Shannon to support my identity, for my imaginary man to fit an unrealistic ideal that I held from childhood, for my selfishness, materialism, and sinful ways to fill my voids, and for love to be based only on what I received. As a Christian mentor who now helps other women in their marriages, I see these same mistakes of unrealistic expectations causing havoc in other families. This has led me to understand that no one can ever be fully prepared to share a lifetime with another person or be ready for the many troubles that life can bring if they begin a marriage and attempt to build a family life based on unrealistic expectations.

We all have our own preferences that differ. Men and women are not made as clones; we do not do everything identically because we think differently. We choose our own priorities based on what we value the most. Just because our husband's or children's priorities may differ from our own does not mean they do not care, or that they don't love us. We all have our own ways of expressing our love for one another. We should allow our husbands and other family members the freedom of uniquely expressing their love without necessarily filling our unique expectations.

Expectations are like chasing the wind. We may think we have it all under control when we set the bar for our husband, child, or other family member to meet our so-called "basic needs", but when they fail to live up to them, our disappointment is inevitable. Our own ideas of love elude us when we aren't being realistic. It is often our own expectations that fail us more than others do.

There is no freedom left for husbands, children, wives or parents when we expect them to do exactly what we want them to do. We cannot try to control them like puppets, and then expect to find our respect for them. Only in fairytales

262

do we have the picture of the seemingly perfect husband and family, where our every wish is their command. Real life is not a fairytale. Other people will always find a way to fail our expectations. When we have realistic expectations of others that they fail to fulfill, we should pray about them to be sure the desires are truly God's will. We should communicate our expectations clearly and ultimately put our hope and trust in God to meet all our needs. He will never reject us when we go to Him. We can depend on Him completely. Trust in God requires us to rely on Him to intervene in our relationships instead of trying to force others to do what we want. The best thing we can do is pray for others and accept them as they truly are. I have learned that if I don't get what I want from others, God must have something better planned, and that allows me to have peace and joy.

The last thing I want to do is end this book by leading women to think that life or marriage is ever going to be exactly what they expect. This is simply not true. Unrealistic expectations can lead to discontentment that may cause the urge to escape from important relationships. There comes a point in time when we must realize that we are to take full responsibility for our own personal joy and happiness. We must stop relying on others to fulfill our vacant souls. Some of us are so busy expecting others to change that we fail to realize our own serious need of change in attitude and behavior. Although we may need to confront certain bad behaviors in others, we must avoid constantly finding their faults and trying to control them. Allowing God to change us gives better results than trying to change anyone else.

I have experienced how expectations can destroy lives. My unrealistic expectations led me to know what it is like to have the kind of despair that paralyzes good decision making. I have experienced the degree of hopelessness from unmet expectations that causes a woman to give up on trying to do what is right in the eyes of God. I understand how expecting others to always be there for me caused torturous loneliness that left me longing for anyone, including the wrong people, to understand me. I have felt emotional pain so badly from the voids of unmet expectations that it propelled me to seek a destructive escape from misery. I experienced the agony of what it was like to act out of desperation because I saw no hope in my future. I once built-up so many negative thoughts about my life and yearned for a promise of relief from a broken heart that felt unbearable. I had nothing left, but a soul full of wounds, bruises, and pain. At the lowest point in life, I found that I could not even live up to my own expectations, much less anyone else's. Unable to find the answers myself and having lost any hope that this world could save me, my desperation found the love of God. It turned out that His unconditional love was the one and only true expectation I could completely rely on.

When I returned to my husband to love him, I did so unknowing what would lie ahead for us. When I sought to re-establish my relationship with my daughter Shannon, I did not know what form it would take or how it would work out. When I gave my life to Jesus, I trusted that He had a plan for my life, although I did not know exactly where it would lead me. When I finally found out who I was, and no longer relied on others for my identity, I did so through faith in Christ. I knew in my heart that repenting for my sins and accepting the love of God was the path to finding my own personal joy and purpose. All of this was done without any of my own expectations, only that God loved me and knew me better than I did myself. It was God's will that I sought in all of this, and no longer my own.

My faithful obedience to God played the major role in the restoration of my life. My identity was set before me as a seeker of biblical truth. I laid my life down to do what I believe God wanted, and my happiness had absolutely nothing to do with any expectations of what would happen upon my return home. My only hope was that I could learn to love my husband and family no matter what sacrifices of selfishness I had to make. Although I was hopeful that we would come to that place where I dreamed of, and that I could delight in my family's love for me as well, this was not the motive for my return. My goal was to experience true love and find it deep within myself to give to others without demanding that love should be returned to me. Scripture does not suggest anywhere that I needed my family's love in return to be fulfilled. It speaks about denying self and holiness being greater than the feelings of happiness. It offered lessons about humility and considering others above myself. God's word encouraged me to love, listen, and bear burdens to the benefit others.

Being free to love, even when things would not be perfect, was more important to me than anything else. I wanted to be free of fearing the outcome of my life and trust that God had the answers I needed. I wanted to take control of my emotions and expectations according to biblical truth and finally be a stable woman. I no longer wanted my unrealistic expectations or the feelings from it to destroy me. My identity had everything to do with holding onto my faith, and following through with what God wanted in everything, no matter how hard it was for my flesh.

Every day since my return home has been filled with new discoveries about myself and my relationships. It has given me plenty of opportunities to do things differently than before. I do not want the same life that I previously had because of the broken woman I was. No longer expecting my family to fulfill my constant need for validation has helped me form the positive core beliefs about myself that I desperately lacked for so long. I realized the irrational amount of value that I placed on my relationships to boost the confidence that I lacked caused us all to suffer greatly.

My healing has done more than benefit myself and my family. It seems that God always has a plan that is bigger than what we could ever imagine. I am blessed to be able to share what I so painfully learned with other women, to save them the time and heartache I went through. I have learned that through faith, God's love grows exponentially from the small seed that we begin with to an unimaginable harvest. I would have never believed that my own personal story could help others until God showed me what He had planned. My ultimate mission in life is to be a vehicle for the healing presence of God to restore lives and relationships.

Once lost with many miles between my real identity and my unrealistic expectations, and longing to bridge the great chasm between myself and my family, I found that uniting with God was my only answer. Amid my weakness, I found strength in the opportunity for faith to change ruin to renewal. No matter where I was or how far I had drifted away, I was not out of reach from His infinite and boundless love. God was the answer to my prayers, the restorer of damaged lives, who forever reminds me that He is the cure for a broken heart. I will forever celebrate the miraculous life changes found along my journey, from healing to wholeness, to never giving up … and finding the love we lost.

At long last, I have come back home.

www.ingramcontent.com/pod-product-compliance
Lightning Source LLC
La Vergne TN
LVHW051113080426
835510LV00018B/2014